Debating Animal Rights

Independence Educational Publishers

First published by Independence Educational Publishers

The Studio, High Green

Great Shelford

Cambridge CB22 5EG

England

© Independence 2016

ISBN-13: 978 1 86168 748 7

Printed in Great Britain
Zenith Print Group

Contents

Introduction

Debating Animal Rights is Volume 303 in the **ISSUES** series. The aim of the series is to offer current, diverse information about important issues in our world, from a UK perspective.

ABOUT DEBATING ANIMAL RIGHTS

'Animal rights' is a topic that never seems to be out of the news. Despite increasingly stringent laws designed to protect animals, horrifying numbers are still subjected to abuse and maltreatment. This book looks at the rights of domestic animals in the UK, but also considers topics such as the responsible use of animals in scientific research. It also explores global animal rights issues, such as the personhood of chimpanzees and the use of elephants at tourist spots in Asia.

OUR SOURCES

Titles in the **ISSUES** series are designed to function as educational resource books, providing a balanced overview of a specific subject.

The information in our books is comprised of facts, articles and opinions from many different sources, including:

⇨ Newspaper reports and opinion pieces

⇨ Website factsheets

⇨ Magazine and journal articles

⇨ Statistics and surveys

⇨ Government reports

⇨ Literature from special interest groups.

A NOTE ON CRITICAL EVALUATION

Because the information reprinted here is from a number of different sources, readers should bear in mind the origin of the text and whether the source is likely to have a particular bias when presenting information (or when conducting their research). It is hoped that, as you read about the many aspects of the issues explored in this book, you will critically evaluate the information presented.

It is important that you decide whether you are being presented with facts or opinions. Does the writer give a biased or unbiased report? If an opinion is being expressed, do you agree with the writer? Is there potential bias to the 'facts' or statistics behind an article?

ASSIGNMENTS

In the back of this book, you will find a selection of assignments designed to help you engage with the articles you have been reading and to explore your own opinions. Some tasks will take longer than others and there is a mixture of design, writing and research-based activities that you can complete alone or in a group.

FURTHER RESEARCH

At the end of each article we have listed its source and a website that you can visit if you would like to conduct your own research. Please remember to critically evaluate any sources that you consult and consider whether the information you are viewing is accurate and unbiased.

Useful weblinks

www.ad-international.org

www.animalsasia.org

www.belfasttelegraph.co.uk

www.birdlife.org

www.theconversation.com

EurActiv.com

www.frame.org.uk

www.gov.uk

www.theguardian.com

www.huffingtonpost.co.uk

www.humanism.org.uk

www.independent.co.uk

www.league.org.uk

www.manchestereveningnews.co.uk

www.mrc.ac.uk

www.pdsa.org.uk

www.politics.co.uk

www.rspca.org.uk

www.yougov.co.uk

www.wessexscene.co.uk

Animal welfare legislation: protecting pets

Guidance and legislation covering pet welfare and animal cruelty.

Animal Welfare Act 2006

The Animal Welfare Act 2006 is the principal animal welfare legislation.

Under the Animal Welfare Act 2006, powers exist for secondary legislation and codes of practice to be made to promote the welfare of animals. The Government is considering a number of specific issues including updating or bringing in new regulations or codes. Until such new provisions are made, existing laws will continue to apply.

Codes of practice

There are codes of practice for the welfare of dogs, cats, horses (including other equidae) and privately kept non-human primates. They provide owners and keepers with information on how to meet the welfare needs of their animals, as required under the Animal Welfare Act 2006. They can also be used in courts as evidence in cases brought before them relating to poor welfare. The codes apply to England only (Wales and Scotland have their own equivalent codes), and are in force from 6 April 2010.

The Performing Animals (Regulation) Act 1925

The welfare of performing animals is provided for in the general provisions to avoid suffering and ensure welfare in the Animal Welfare Act 2006. In addition the training and exhibition of performing animals is further regulated by the 1925 act which requires trainers and exhibitors of such animals to be registered with the local authority.

Under this act, the police and officers of local councils, who may include a vet, have power to enter premises where animals are being trained and exhibited, and if cruelty and neglect are detected, magistrates' courts can prohibit or restrict the training or exhibition of the animals and suspend or cancel the registration granted under the act. Under this act councils are required to send copies of any certificates to Defra.

The Pet Animals Act 1951 (as amended in 1983)

This act protects the welfare of animals sold as pets. It requires any person keeping a pet shop to be licensed by the local council.

Before granting a licence the council must be satisfied that:

⇨ the animals are kept in accommodation that is both suitable and clean

⇨ they are supplied with appropriate food and drink

⇨ are adequately protected from disease and fire.

The local council may attach any conditions to the licence, may inspect the licensed premises at all reasonable times and may refuse a licence if the conditions at the

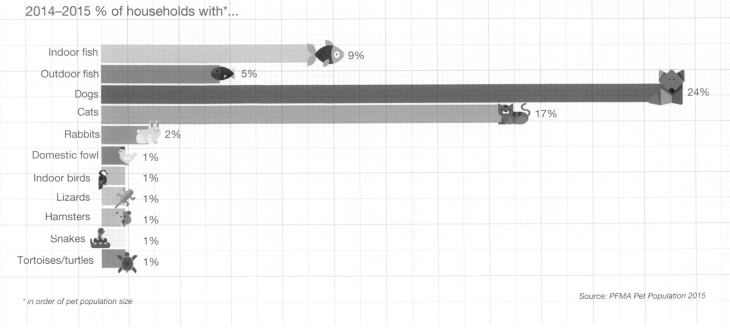

2014–2015 % of households with*...

Indoor fish	9%
Outdoor fish	5%
Dogs	24%
Cats	17%
Rabbits	2%
Domestic fowl	1%
Indoor birds	1%
Lizards	1%
Hamsters	1%
Snakes	1%
Tortoises/turtles	1%

*in order of pet population size

Source: PFMA Pet Population 2015

premises are unsatisfactory or if the terms of the licence are not being complied with.

Councils are responsible for enforcing the law in this area and anyone who has reason to believe that a pet shop is keeping animals in inadequate conditions should raise the matter with the council who will decide what action to take within the range of its powers.

Under section 2 of this act, pets cannot be sold in the street, including on barrows and markets.

Animal Boarding Establishments Act 1963

Establishments where the boarding of animals is being carried on as a business are subject to the 1963 act, which requires such establishments to be licensed by the local council. For the purpose of this act the keeping of such establishments is defined as the carrying on at any premises, including a private dwelling, of a business of providing accommodation for other people's cats and dogs.

The licence is granted at the discretion of the local council which may take into account the suitability of the accommodation and whether the animals are well fed, exercised and protected from disease and fire.

Riding Establishments Act 1964 and 1970

Riding establishments are licensed by local councils under the 1964 act. The council can impose conditions on the licence. The council, in the exercise of its discretion, may take into account:

⇨ the suitability of the applicant or manager

⇨ the accommodation and pasture

⇨ adequacy of the provision for the horses' health, welfare and exercise

⇨ precautions against fire and disease

⇨ suitability of the horses with regards to the reasons they are being kept.

Breeding and Sale of Dogs (Welfare) Act 1999, Breeding of Dogs Act 1991 and Breeding of Dogs Act 1973

The Breeding and Sale of Dogs (Welfare) Act 1999, which amended and extended the provisions of the Breeding of Dogs Act 1973 and the Breeding of Dogs Act 1991, already provides protection for dogs used in breeding establishments.

Under this legislation, any person who keeps a breeding establishment for dogs at any premises and carries on at those premises a business of breeding dogs for sale must obtain a licence from the local council. Those people who are not in the business of breeding dogs for sale, so-called "hobby breeders", and produce less than five litters in any period of 12 months do not need a licence.

The local council has the discretion whether to grant a licence and, before doing so, must satisfy itself that:

⇨ the animals are provided with suitable accommodation, food, water and bedding material

⇨ are adequately exercised and visited at suitable intervals

⇨ all reasonable precautions are taken to prevent and control the spread of diseases amongst dogs

Local councils are responsible for enforcing the legislation.

In addition to ensuring that dogs are kept in suitable accommodation, the law also places limits on the frequency and timing of breeding from a bitch. Bitches cannot be mated before they are a year old, must have no more than six litters in a lifetime and can only have one litter every 12 months.

Breeding records must be kept to ensure that these requirements are adhered to. Puppies that are produced at licensed breeding establishments can only be sold at those premises or a licensed pet shop.

Updated 18 April 2013

⇨ The above information is reprinted with kind permission from the Department for Environment, Food & Rural Affairs. Please visit www.gov.uk for further information.

RSPCA shocked at staggering numbers of animals trafficked into UK from EU

The RSPCA has called for Westminster Government to tackle the illegal trade in puppies after new figures revealed an increase in the number of dogs being imported into the UK from EU countries.

Defra announced on Thursday (21 January) the number of dogs trafficked into the country for commercial and non-commercial reasons in 2015. And the statistics reveal that imports from Ireland, Lithuania, Hungary, Poland and Romania – all countries identified as having large scale puppy farm operations – have risen by 75%.

In October 2015, the RSPCA launched its Scrap the Puppy Trade campaign to tackle the unscrupulous puppy breeders and traders operating in England, as well as those importing from overseas.

The charity is concerned about the way many puppies are bred and sold like commodities with little or no regard to their future well-being. Some puppies die prematurely or develop behavioural or health problems as a result of poor breeding.

The Society is calling on the Westminster Government to develop legislation which tackles the root causes of the problem, including cutting off the trade in illegally imported puppies from Europe with increased enforcement at our borders and with increased accountability and monitoring for anyone breeding puppies.

The figures show that while imports of dogs from non-UK EU countries rose by 7%, imports from those five countries rose by 75%. And 38% of all dogs imported to the UK come from the five countries where puppy farming operates on a large scale: Lithuania, Hungary, Romania, Poland and Ireland.

That means of the 93,424 dogs imported to the UK in 2015, 33,249 came from one of these five.

David Bowles, the RSPCA's head of public affairs, said: "We are appalled by the figures released by Defra, which show the shocking scale of this problem.

"What is particularly concerning is the number of animals coming into the UK from countries such as Romania and Ireland, where we know puppy farmers and breeders are trying to cash in on the demand for certain dog breeds here in the UK.

"Many of the thousands of dogs coming into this country every year may well have started their life in appalling conditions on a puppy farm."

David added: "While there is a demand for cheap, pure-bred and fashionable crossbreed puppies, breeders, dealers and traders will find a way to sell them.

"Puppy trafficking is big business, with dealers exploiting the current lack of enforcement at our ports and making huge profits bringing in large numbers of highly sought after puppies.

"Many buyers won't be aware in what conditions their puppy has been bred and raised nor where their puppy has come from. They are effectively buying blind.

"Many of the puppies being imported are too young to have been removed from their mothers and have not been vaccinated against disease. Some puppies die in transit and many fall sick or die shortly after purchase, leaving their owners heartbroken and lumbered with huge vet bills.

"We believe that if we are to seriously tackle the poor breeding and illegal trade in puppies, the tap needs to be switched off. We need to see an overhaul of current legislation and improved enforcement which tackles the root causes of the problem."

Commercial and non-commercial imports from Romania in 2015 rose by a staggering 88% from the previous year. The country is the largest exporter of dogs to the UK, with 10,800 coming into the country last year.

Imports from Ireland are now finally being declared and are at their highest, with more than 10,000 entering the UK in 2015.

Meanwhile, non-UK EU imports have risen by 7% and commercial imports also rose by 7%.

The RSPCA is asking members of the public to support our Scrap the Puppy Trade campaign and sign our petition at www.rspca.org.uk/scrapthepuppytrade to tell Westminster that puppies are more precious than pieces of metal and to bring in new legislation to tackle puppy imports and the puppy trade in England.

Notes to editors

⇨ 93,424 animals were imported into the UK in 2015 for commercial and non-commercial reasons.

⇨ 85,730 animals were imported into the UK in 2015 from within the EU.

⇨ 33,249 animals were imported into the UK in 2015 from Ireland, Lithuania, Hungary, Poland and Romania – that's up 75% (14,339) from 18,910 in 2014.

25 January 2016

⇨ The above information is reprinted with kind permission from politics.co.uk. Please visit www.politics.co.uk for further information.

BBC *Panorama*: *Britain's Puppy Dealers Exposed* reveals the shocking truth behind puppy farms

"We shouldn't be farming dogs on a mass scale."

By Kathryn Snowdon

Undercover footage from a BBC *Panorama* investigation into puppy farms reveals the "ruthless world" of the lucrative industry.

Britain's Puppy Dealers Exposed, which airs on Monday night, will see reporter Samantha Poling tracking the supply chain of Britain's favourite pet.

Recordings from inside Irish puppy mills show scores of breeding dogs being kept in ramshackle cages, with water supplied to them by pipes that are normally seen in battery pig farming.

Marc Abraham, vet and founder of Pup Aid, which campaigns to end puppy farming, told *Panorama*: "This is an industry built on lack of transparency, deceit, cruelty and animal suffering."

The multi-million pound puppy breeding business has come under increased scrutiny in recent months.

Last year the RSPCA launched its Scrap The Puppy Trade campaign in a bid to tackle the trafficking of sick dogs.

The RSPCA believes that huge numbers of puppies are being trafficked into the country from other EU countries to meet the high demand for pedigree and designer crossbred puppies in the UK.

A report released by Battersea Dogs and Cats Home in October revealed how the unregulated breeding industry was putting dogs at risk.

The London-based rehoming centre's report showed that less than 12% of puppies in the UK are bred by licensed breeders, meaning that dogs could be sold from unsuitable premises, long before they are ready to leave their mothers.

BBC reporter Poling spent six months investigating the darker side of the puppy trade.

Secret filming at Raymond Cullivan's puppy farm in County Cavan, Republic of Ireland, shows dogs giving birth in confined spaces, unable to move around freely.

These boxes, which offer little or no ventilation or daylight, provide no space away from the pups, are illegal in Ireland.

Yet despite such breaches of animal welfare legislation, many of these pups are bound for the UK market.

Eric Hale's beagles are Kennel Club registered and have qualified for Crufts in the past. Poling describes him as "one of Britain's most prolific dog dealers".

Every Tuesday he loads his van with crates of pups, travels by boat to Liverpool and drives around the country dropping dogs off to the next link in the supply chain.

From large-scale sellers, to country layby dealers, Hale delivers to all, Poling says.

She adds: "Hale is in the big league. We discovered he was licensed for 120 breeding bitches.

"With a puppy farm of that size, it's harder to control disease and give each dog the human attention it needs if it's to be a happy family pet."

The reporter films in secret at Hale's puppy farm at 2am. It is minus six degrees and the team records using night vision cameras.

Poling says that the behaviour of the dogs is "disturbing to watch".

Many of the dogs have little or no bedding and, after watching the farm for several days saw, she no sign of the dogs being routinely taken out of the barns.

Hale said in a statement that his kennels met "all the requirements for a breeding establishment".

Animal legislation experts told the BBC programme the facilities did not provide adequate barriers to prevent disease and that the dogs were "basically in jail" and "seriously deprived".

Poling said that most of the puppies end up being sold online by dealers who will often try to hide where the dogs have come from, with adverts implying the dogs have been born and brought up in a family home.

Abraham said: "In 2016, we should be better than this. We shouldn't be farming dogs on a mass scale.

"They feel pain, they feel suffering, they feel fear.

"The only people benefiting are the irresponsible breeders and the dog dealers."

16 May 2016

⇨ The above information is reprinted with kind permission from The Huffington Post UK. Please visit www.huffingtonpost.co.uk for further information.

Bullfighting row: Ricky Gervais lashes out against controversial sport as another man dies

By Eve Hartley

A matador has been gored to death by a bull after taking part in an annual summer festival in Spain, sparking a furious outcry from ardent animal rights activist and comedian Ricky Gervais.

The incident, which occurred in Lerin, northern Spain, was caught on video and saw Miguel Ruiz Perez struck in the abdomen after slipping as he took part in a spectacle involving athletes and bulls.

The fighter was trapped between the bull and the wooden fence for several seconds before he could be treated by the medical team, who rushed on to stretcher him out of the arena.

Perez lost his footing after circling the animal in the sandy arena, which led the bull to quickly pounce, ploughing into him with its horns.

The death of Perez took the number of bull-related deaths to four in just three days at summer festivals across the country.

Local authorities are currently deciding whether to suspend the week-long town festival.

Gervais lead the charge on Twitter to voice his disgust at the sport: "Neither I nor any bull wants you to fight it. But if you insist I hope it defends itself. F*** anyone who tortures an animal for fun," he said.

Gervais also posted a video in which he said: "I mean the truth is I do prefer the bull to win.

"I'd rather you didn't fight a bull, but if you do – if you choose to torture an animal to death for fun – I hope it defends itself and self defence is no offence."

He continued: "Who wants to torture an animal to death? And what morons go and watch it?"

"It's terrified already – the crowds shouting – it's disorientated, it just wants it to stop. It's done nothing wrong, this bull."

"If you choose to fight a bull for fun – f*** you."

The death toll of bull attacks now stands at seven people since the beginning of July, four of them over the past weekend.

Last year more than 7,200 bulls and steers (castrated bull calves) were killed by bullfighters across Spain, the news website El Diario reports.

17 August 2015

⇨ The above information is reprinted with kind permission from The Huffington Post UK. Please visit www.huffingtonpost.co.uk for further information.

Denmark bans kosher and halal slaughter as minister says "animal rights come before religion"

New law, denounced as "anti-Semitism" by Jewish leaders, comes after country controversially slaughtered a giraffe in public and fed him to lions.

By Adam Withnall

Denmark's government has brought in a ban on the religious slaughter of animals for the production of halal and kosher meat, after years of campaigning from welfare activists.

The change to the law, announced last week and effective as of yesterday, has been called "anti-Semitism" by Jewish leaders and "a clear interference in religious freedom" by the non-profit group Danish Halal.

European regulations require animals to be stunned before they are slaughtered, but grants exemptions on religious grounds. For meat to be considered kosher under Jewish law or halal under Islamic law, the animal must be conscious when killed.

Yet defending his government's decision to remove this exemption, the minister for agriculture and food Dan Jørgensen told Denmark's TV2 that "animal rights come before religion".

Commenting on the change, Israel's deputy minister of religious services

Rabbi Eli Ben Dahan told *The Jewish Daily Forward*: "European anti-Semitism is showing its true colours across Europe, and is even intensifying in the government institutions."

Al Jazeera quoted the monitoring group Danish Halal, which launched a petition against the ban, as saying it was "a clear interference in religious freedom limiting the rights of Muslims and Jews to practise their religion in Denmark".

The ban has divided opinions in the country, particularly after it recently made headlines for animal welfare policy after Copenhagen Zoo slaughtered the "surplus" young male giraffe Marius.

On Twitter, David Krikler (@davekriks) wrote: "In Denmark butchering a healthy giraffe in front of kids is cool but a kosher/halal chicken is illegal."

Byakuya Ali-Hassan (@SirOthello) said it was "disgusting" that "the same country that slaughtered a giraffe in public to be fed to lions...

is banning halal meat because of the procedures".

Mogens Larsen (@Moq72), from Aalborg in Denmark, tweeted: "Denmark bans the religious slaughter of animals. Not even zoo lions are allowed a taste of halal giraffe."

Last year politicians in Britain said they would not be outlawing religious slaughter despite "strong pressure" from the RSPCA, the National Secular Society and other activists.

18 February 2014

⇨ The above information is reprinted with kind permission from *The Independent*. Please visit www.independent.co.uk for further information.

European Commission survey finds widespread support for clearer labelling for meat from non-stunned animals

The British Humanist Association (BHA) has renewed its calls for labelling of meat from animals which have not been not pre-stunned, following a European Commission (EC) survey which found overwhelming consumer demand for clearer meat labelling. 72% of consumers surveyed indicated their interest in "receiving information on the stunning of animals at slaughter when they buy meat". The BHA gave oral evidence to the Commission's scoping exercise which led to the report in which the survey is contained.

In the UK, animal welfare laws require food animals to be pre-stunned before slaughter, but exemptions exist to this for certain religious communities. As a result, all meat produced by the *shechita* (kosher) method and around 20% of halal is not pre-stunned. The EC's report found that consumers had very limited understanding of these processes, and were unable to make clear ethical decisions about which meat they purchased.

A potential move towards meat labelling is supported by the Halal Food Authority, the British Veterinary Association, the Royal Society for the Prevention of Cruelty to Animals, and the Farm Animal Welfare Council, but has been strenuously opposed by some Muslim and Jewish pressure groups.

BHA Director of Public Affairs and Campaigns Pavan Dhaliwal commented, "The evidence is clear and uncontroversial: pre-stunning significantly reduces the distress experienced by animals used for meat production. This latest European Commission report shows that there is both widespread demand and clear need for labelling of meat. This is a very modest measure, and while we ultimately hope that slaughter without stunning is brought to an end, in the meantime we hope our politicians will look at the evidence and choose to empower consumers to make informed decisions about which foods they buy."

9 June 2015

United Kingdom monthly numbers of livestock slaughtered				thousand head
	July 2015	**May 2016**	**June 2016**	**July 2016**	yr on yr
	35 days	31 days	30 days	31 days	% change*
Steers	93	80	82	83	0.8
Heifers	62	56	57	58	4.7
Young bulls	27	20	24	27	122
Cows & adult bulls	56	46	48	53	5.1
Calves (1)	7	8	8	7	18
Clean sheep	1289	853	1000	1127	-1.3
Ewes and rams	151	127	135	137	2.7
Clean pigs	1003	857	863	891	0.3
Sows and boars	23	21	23	19	-8.6

(1) The definition of calves from May 2014 is 'Bovines less than one year'.

* Calculated using an average daily throughout each month

The above table shows monthly estimates of the number of home killed cattle, sheep and pigs, slaughtered as meat for human consumption in UK abattoirs. From February 2016 onwards, the survey is run according to calendar rather than statistical months. To allow a direct comparison with 2015 data which was based on a statistical month, the number of days in each period is specified below and comparisons are based on average daily throughput in the month.

Source: Department for Environment Food & Rural Affairs, United Kingdom Slaughter Statistics – July 2016

⇨ The above information is reprinted with kind permission from the British Humanist Association. Please visit www.humanism.org.uk for further information.

A dog fight every day – new report exposes extent of 'banned' sport in UK

A new report into dog fighting – Betrayal of Trust: The Tragedy of Dog Fighting – reveals at least one dog fight is likely to take place every day of the year somewhere in the UK despite the barbaric 'sport' having been outlawed almost 200 years ago.

Commissioned by the League Against Cruel Sports, the report is the first comprehensive look at dog fighting in the UK, and also highlights:

⇨ Three distinct 'levels' of dog fighting: Street Rolls, Hobbyist and Professional

⇨ Horrific injuries patched up by 'street' surgeons using only superglue or staples

⇨ Training methods using 'bait' animals such as cats

⇨ Organised dog fights that can last up to five hours.

The authors of the report, criminologists Dr Simon Harding and Dr Angus Nurse spoke to a large range of people including those involved in dog fighting, and examined the practices, motivations and extent of dog fighting as well as the means to tackle it.

Mark McCormick, Head of Campaigns for League Against Cruel Sports said: "The UK's dog lovers will be sickened to learn that the cruelty of dogfighting, which can result in torn flesh, blood loss, disembowelment or even death, continues to go on in this country.

"Traditionally dog fighting was hidden away in rural areas and managed almost to a professional level. Now we're seeing a move to urban areas, where dog fighting is becoming a way of establishing dominance, often related to gang activity. Either way, it's often about machismo and money, and the dogs will inevitably suffer."

The three levels of dog fighting identified in the report are:

Level one: street rolls

⇨ One-on-one fights in urban parks and housing estates

⇨ Arranged on the spot, no referee or rules, fight over in a few minutes

⇨ Little or no money involved

⇨ Likely to occur somewhere in the UK every day

Level two: hobbyist

⇨ Series of fights in abandoned buildings/bedrooms converted into a 'pit'

⇨ Operate on a localised fighting circuit in urban areas

⇨ Often gang affiliated with gambling involved

⇨ Likely to occur somewhere in the UK every couple of weeks

Level three: professional

⇨ Sophisticated dog rings with highly trained dogs of reputable bloodlines

⇨ Always take place in a pit, with rules, referees, timekeepers, spectators

⇨ High stakes gambling with £100,000s wagered

⇨ Dogs entered in fights both in UK and internationally

⇨ Likely to occur somewhere in UK every few months

Dr Simon Harding, author of the report, and Senior Lecturer in Criminology in Middlesex University's School of Law said: "From our interviews with people who involve their dogs in fighting, and analysing data from a wide range of sources, we found clear evidence of dog fighting in the UK ranging from the everyday impromptu street fights or 'rolls', through hobbyists to professional fights where huge amounts of money changes hand.

"It is clear that regardless of the level of dog fighting, these people are all connected by a common thread of secrecy, callousness and links to other crimes."

Dr Harding continued: "Dog fighting is a cruel and violent practice which has no place in 21st-century Britain. Offenders take ordinary animals, manipulate and exploit them for profit and reputational gain. It is a serious concern that this activity, outlawed 180 years ago, remains, and in some communities, thrives even today. We should all work together to eradicate this practice once and for all."

Pain and suffering

The suffering of the dogs involved not only includes the pain – and sometimes death – inflicted during the fights themselves, but also from brutal training methods, particularly at the Professional level. Dogs reared for fighting are engineered so they are robbed entirely of their natural social behaviour and designed to fight regardless of pain or risk.

Mark McCormick adds: "As a visit to the vet would lead to awkward questions, fighting dogs are often denied proper medical attention and horrific injuries are left to be patched up with superglue or staples, often with fatal consequences."

Links to other crimes

From analysing data provided by the Metropolitan Police and other sources, the report identified that young men who owned 'dangerous dogs' or 'status dogs', as defined under the Dangerous Dogs Act, were widely associated with or involved in an extensive range of criminal activity, including robbery, threats to kill, actual bodily harm and drug possession.

On Merseyside, 23 out of 25 dangerous dog owners had 87 convictions amongst them, while in the West Midlands 79 out of the 126 dangerous dog owners had other criminal convictions.

The law

The specific offence of dog fighting does not exist in the UK; it is contained within the broader offence of animal fighting prohibited under Section 8 of the Animal Welfare Act with a maximum penalty of 51 weeks in prison.

By contrast, in the US dog fighting is a felony offence in all 50 states with a maximum penalty of several years in prison. But because of the clandestine nature of the activity, it is very difficult to obtain convictions.

Mark McCormick added: "Disappointingly low conviction rates highlight the difficulties of enforcing the law when it comes to such a clandestine activity and we believe more resources and research into the problem is essential. In addition, we are recommending measures that could help make the law on dogfighting more enforceable, including the mandatory recording of dog fighting offences and strengthening penalties to bring them into line with other European countries"

8 December 2015

⇨ The above information is reprinted with kind permission from the League Against Cruel Sports. Please visit www.league.org.uk for further information.

25 million birds illegally slaughtered in the Mediterranean every year

Unlawfully shot, trapped or glued: tens of millions of birds are being killed illegally each year across the Mediterranean, according to the first scientific review of its kind to be carried out in the region by BirdLife International.

BirdLife and Partners have uncovered the shocking extent to which a number of birds are being illegally killed, putting together a list of the ten countries with the highest estimated annual death toll.

Although countries currently hit by conflict, such as Syria and Libya, feature high in the rankings, some European nations also fare poorly.

Italy (where 5.6 million birds are estimated to be killed illegally every year[1]) is second only to Egypt for the estimated mean number of illegal killings each year, with the Famagusta area of Cyprus the single worst location in the Mediterranean.[2]

Other European countries featuring in the top ten are; Greece (mean estimate of 0.7 million birds killed annually[3]), France (0.5 million[4]), Croatia (0.5 million[5]) and Albania (0.3 million[6]).

This further demonstrates why the Birds Directive, currently under review by the European Commission, should be better implemented, rather than re-opened.

Despite not ranking in the top ten overall, Malta (where 108,000 birds are estimated to be killed illegally each year[7]) is still seeing the region's highest estimated number of birds illegally killed per square kilometre.

The review also exposes some of the common methods of killing in use across the Mediterranean, including illegal shooting, capture in nets and recordings of bird sounds used to lure large numbers of birds to illegal trapping locations.

Many of the cruel methods used, such as lime sticks that glue the birds to branches, cause considerable suffering before resulting in the bird's death.

The report estimates that Eurasian Chaffinch comes top of the 'kill list' (an estimated 2.9 million are killed each year[8]), with Eurasian Blackcap (1.8 million[9]), Common Quail (1.6 million[10]) and Song Thrush (1.2 million[11]) making up the rest of the top four.

A number of species, such as Eurasian Curlew, already listed as 'Near Threatened' or 'Vulnerable' on the International Union for Conservation of Nature's Red List are also in danger.

The review's publication comes ahead of Birdfair 2015, which gets underway today [Friday 21 August 2015] at Rutland Water Nature Reserve in the UK.

It also marks the launch of BirdLife's new Keeping the Flyway Safe fundraising campaign to help target resources for conservation in the worst affected locations.

BirdLife International CEO, Patricia Zurita, stated: "This review shows the gruesome extent to which birds are being killed illegally in the Mediterranean. Populations of some species that were once abundant in Europe are declining, with a number even in free-fall and disappearing altogether."

"Our birds deserve safer flyways – concluded BirdLife's CEO – and we want conservation efforts to be increased now, before it's too late."

The data in this review previews a scientific paper due to be published soon giving a full assessment of the situation in the Mediterranean.[12]

21 August 2015

⇨ Information reprinted with kind permission from Bird Life International. Visit www.birdlife.org for further information.

Notes for editors
(1) Italy: the mean estimated number of birds killed illegally each year is 5.6 million, with a minimum number of 3.4 million and maximum number of 7.8 million.
(2) Cyprus – the mean estimated number of birds killed illegally each year in the Famagusta region is 689,000, with a minimum of 405,000 and a maximum of 974,000.
(3) Greece: the mean estimated number of birds killed illegally each year is 704,000, with a minimum of 485,000 and maximum number of 922,000.
(4) France: the mean estimated number of birds killed illegally each year is 522,000, with a minimum of 149,000 and maximum number of 895,000.
(5) Croatia: the mean estimated number of birds killed illegally each year is 510,000, with a minimum of 166,000 and maximum number of 855,000.
(6) Albania: the mean estimated number of birds killed illegally each year is 265,000, with a minimum of 206,000 and maximum number of 325,000.
(7) Malta: the mean estimated number of birds killed illegally each year is 108,000, with a minimum of 5,600 and a maximum of 211,000.
(8) Eurasian Chaffinch – the mean estimated number killed illegally each year is 2.9 million, with a minimum number of 2.2 million and a maximum number of 3.6 million.
(9) Eurasian Blackcap – the mean estimated number killed illegally each year is 1.8 million, with a minimum number of 1.2 million and a maximum number of 2.4 million.
(10) Common Quail – the mean estimated number killed illegally each year is 1.6 million, with a minimum number of 1.0 million and a maximum number of 2.2 million.
(11) Song thrush – the mean estimated number killed illegally each year is 1.2 million, with a minimum number of 0.7 million and a maximum number of 1.7 million.
(12) All numbers are best estimates, for further details and minimum/maximum estimates, see the scientific paper: Preliminary assessment of the scope and scale of illegal killing and taking of birds in the Mediterranean (Brochet et al., in revision).

New circus ban bill provides fresh hope for wild animals

Anew bill to ban wild animals in English circuses could provide long-suffering circus animals with the reprieve they desperately need.

Please contact your MP today and urge them to support The Wild Animals in Circuses (Prohibition) Bill which will have its next second reading on Friday 11 March 2016 (the first being blocked on 4 March).

Will Quince, MP for Colchester (Conservative) who introduced the new bill on Wednesday 10 February 2016 said: "The use of wild animals in travelling circuses can no longer be justified. Circuses can never recreate the natural habitat of a wild species. What's more, there is no longer any educational, conservational nor research benefit from using wild animals solely for spectacle.

"The majority of the public supports a ban, as do most MPs. I hope we follow the lead of many of our European neighbours and ban the use of wild animals in circuses once and for all."

Although the Government claims that it remains committed to its 2012 promise, and manifesto pledge, to end what the Prime Minister has called an "outdated practice", little progress has been made. Announcing the proposed ban four years ago, the Government said the legislation could "help ensure that our international reputation as a leading protector of animals continues into a new global era". Britain now lags behind more than 30 countries around the world that have already restricted the use of wild animals in circuses.

Without prohibitive legislation there could be an increase in wild animal acts and a new big cat circus is already poised to return to England. Fronted by Thomas Chipperfield, the show was prevented from touring last year after an inspection found the living conditions for the lions and tigers to be inadequate.

Changing attitudes and awareness of animal suffering have seen the number of wild animal circuses plummet. Only two circuses now perform in England with wild animals, Circus Mondao and Peter Jolly's Circus, who are licensed under a temporary scheme introduced by the Government ahead of the ban. ADI evidence has shown that inspections have not safeguarded welfare or protected animals from abuse.

Once a UK measure is passed, ADI has offered to assist with the relocation of circus animals, should the need arise. We are currently working with authorities in Peru and Colombia to enforce similar legislation and have rescued and relocated over 100 animals during our 18-month Operation Spirit of Freedom mission, with 33 lions soon be airlifted to the Emoya Big Cat Sanctuary in South Africa.

Our shocking revelations in the UK of the brutal violence and constant chaining of Anne the elephant at the Bobby Roberts Super Circus led to the cruelty conviction of her owner under the Animal Welfare Act. As a result MPs demanded action to protect wild animals in circuses.

Our Stop Circus Suffering campaign is supported by celebrities including Ricky Gervais, Dame Judi Dench, Sir Paul McCartney, Sir Roger Moore, Brian May, Moby, Imelda Staunton, Eddie Izzard, Twiggy and Annette Crosbie. Expressing his exasperation at the lack of progress, actor Brian Blessed said last year: "I am deeply opposed to the use of wild animals in circuses and have been working with Animal Defenders International to oppose such acts for many years. Despite repeated promises from the Government, we are still waiting for the law to pass and the animals are continuing to suffer. Please end this circus madness."

4 March 2016

⇨ The above information is reprinted with kind permission from Animal Defenders International. Please visit www.ad-international.org for further information.

Three-quarters of public back ban on pet monkeys

The public overwhelmingly want pet primates banned in Britain and few want one for themselves, but views vary by age.

By Will Jordan

MPs have stopped short of backing a ban on keeping and trading primates (monkeys and apes) as pets, arguing that more research must be done into the number of primate pets already in Britain. Current estimates vary wildly – between 3,000 and 20,000, according to a recent report by the Commons Environment, Food and Rural Affairs Committee. MPs say accurate data is essential to laying the groundwork for establishing a ban, something animal welfare groups already support.

The move is widely backed by public opinion, according to the latest YouGov research. By 75% to 11%, British people say keeping monkeys as pets should be banned.

Views are generally similar across demographics, but there are significant variances among different age groups. Specifically, there is a 31-point gap in support for the ban between 18- to 24-year-olds (54%) and people aged 60 and up (85%).

One possible explanation for the difference: a quarter of people in that younger age group also answer "yes" to the question "would you like a monkey for a pet?" Among

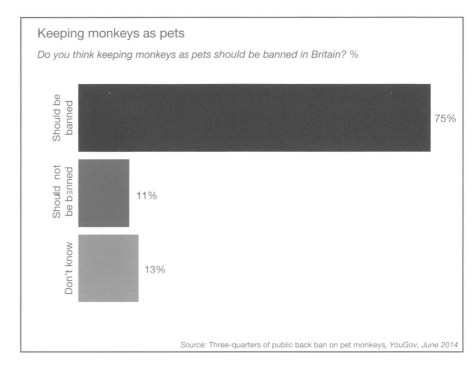

Keeping monkeys as pets

Do you think keeping monkeys as pets should be banned in Britain? %

Source: Three-quarters of public back ban on pet monkeys, YouGov, June 2014

over-60s, that number is barely above zero (3%).

Overall, nine per cent of British people say they would like a monkey for a pet.

Though the MPs express support for the ban in their report, the step is also described as "draconian". Welfare groups argue that the social, behavioural, environmental and dietary needs of primates are too complex to be provided in a domestic environment.

13 June 2014

⇨ The above information is reprinted with kind permission from YouGov. Please visit www.yougov.co.uk for further information.

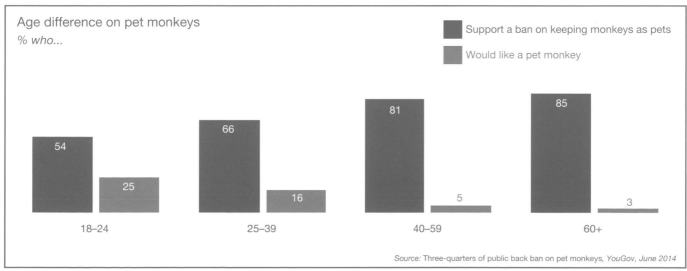

Age difference on pet monkeys
% who...

Support a ban on keeping monkeys as pets

Would like a pet monkey

	18–24	25–39	40–59	60+
Support a ban	54	66	81	85
Would like a pet monkey	25	16	5	3

Source: Three-quarters of public back ban on pet monkeys, YouGov, June 2014

German court rules killing day-old live male chicks does not contravene their animal rights

Male chicks are either killed by gassing or being crushed in a macerator machine.

By Emma Henderson

A German court has ruled the mass killing of day-old male chicks does not violate their animal protection laws.

Male chicks are killed because they are unable to lay eggs and do not put on enough weight to be reared for meat.

The High Administrative Court said the "breeding of male chicks is not in keeping with the stated goal of chicken breeding and its business guidelines."

There are about 30 million hens in the UK who lay eggs. Approximately 66% of these are kept in cages.

It argued the killing of male chicks was "part of the process for providing the population with eggs and meat".

Germany's Animal Protection Law allows for lawful killings of animals providing there is sound economic reason to do so.

Globally, 70–80% of egg-laying hens are kept in battery cages.

The Green Party introduced a bill in the German parliament attempting to ban the process, but parliament voted against it in March.

Following the rulling, one western state in Germany – North Rhine-Westphalia – still wants to ban the killing of male chicks for economic reasons. The state's agricultural minister, Johannes Remmel of the Green party said: "We must finally stop treating animals like garbage."

Animal Aid, a UK animal rights organisation, estimates around 30 million day-old male chicks are disposed of every year in the UK, while worldwide estimates reach 2.5 billion.

The male chicks are either gassed with carbon monoxide or put into a macerating machine which kills them instantly by crushing them. Animal rights activists say the process is the same as mass murder.

The RSPCA lists maceration as one of their permitted method of killing chicks, which also includes gassing and notes chicks must be killed within 15 minutes of being removed from the hatchery.

Germany's national agricultural minister, Bavarian conservative Christian Schmidt wants a "practical alternative to the shredding of chicks by 2017".

He suggests this involves laser technology, which could determine the sex of the egg before it hatches. But judges rejected the idea, ruling this practice was not yet ready.

25 May 2016

⇨ The above information is reprinted with kind permission from *The Independent*. Please visit www.independent.co.uk for further information.

© *independent.co.uk 2016*

The average consumer in the UK eats 170 eggs per year.

Source of infographics: *From shell to hell: the modern egg industry*, Animal Aid, 2016

Animal welfare and animal rights are very different beasts

THE CONVERSATION

An article from **The Conversation.**

By Robert John Young, Professor of Wildlife Conservation, University of Salford

More than 20 years ago, the university department where I was doing my PhD was fire bombed by animal rights activists. At the time, I was conducting research into animal welfare, as were many of the staff in my department. I found it hard to understand why a research department whose main objective was to improve the well-being of animals would be the target for such an attack.

I suspect most people, as I did then, see animal welfare and animal rights as synonyms. In reality, however, they are at opposite ends of the continuum concerning our treatment of animals.

Proponents of animal welfare are interested in questions like: "How can we improve the well-being of zoo animals?" Whereas animal rights supporters ask questions like: "Should we have zoos?"

These are very different questions with diametrically opposed outcomes: the constant improvement of zoos or their closing down. Both could be argued to improve animal well-being, but one is highly pragmatic, whereas the other is philosophical.

Cost-benefit analysis

Accepting and working with the status quo that animals are used for important research or housed in zoos for conservation purposes, my job as an animal welfare scientist is to maximise their well-being in these situations. Much of my work is based on the ideas of the utilitarian philosopher Jeremy Bentham who famously said of animals and their well-being:

"The question is not: 'Can they reason?' Nor: 'Can they talk?' But: 'Can they suffer?'"

Bentham, importantly, put the focus on the practical question of suffering, moving the debate away from human-animal comparisons, and brought in the concept of a cost-benefit analysis.

Human activities affect the well-being of animals to different degrees and society uses Bentham's cost-benefit analysis to determine whether what we are doing is acceptable. For example, treatments for diabetes were developed on animals in laboratories. These animals paid the cost with their lives and, consequently, hundreds of millions of people, presently, benefit from a treatment for a terrible disease. This cost-benefit analysis is enshrined in many laws relating to animal welfare.

The role of animal welfare scientists is, on a practical level, to improve animal well-being. On a philosophical level, it accepts some of the ways that human activity impinges on the well-being of animals and works to minimise their cost and maximise the benefits to them.

From this perspective, it can be argued that animal welfare research justifies the continued use of animals by humans, be it for research, for food or in zoos. The support for the continued use of animals for scientific purposes is a particular

walk?! ... only if you give me a treat...

...REMEMBER WHEN GOING FOR A WALK WAS THE TREAT... ?

cause of conflict with animal rights activists – hence why my university department was fire bombed.

Human concerns

I believe we should do our utmost to improve constantly the conditions of animals affected by human activities. Like animal rights advocates, my concern is to improve the lot of animals. But, while their approach is to abolish the use of animals, my approach is to work with animal industries. We take a pragmatic stance that it is impossible for modern society to function without using animals – be it for food or for medical research.

Most people I suspect have sympathy for the welfare and rights approach, depending on the issue at hand. I, for example, would not support research to improve the wellbeing of whales being hunted for scientific or other purposes. There is, in my opinion, no humane way to kill whales and I disagree with exploiting highly sentient animals when the capacity to suffer seems to be linked to cognitive abilities.

But I have to admit when the use of animals affects my life directly then I am more likely to support an animal welfare approach. In the past few years, several members of my family have had life-threatening conditions and all have survived due to medical care based on research using animals. Therefore my interest in this subject derives from what John Stuart Mills called "enlightened self-interest" – that is, we have a moral obligation to take care of the animals who improve our well-being.

Just like voting for a political party, before you pin your flag to one cause or another be sure you understand the implication of your choice and that you are prepared to live with it. This might be animals being held in imperfect conditions, but conditions that are improving, or a world without zoos and limited medical advances.

20 May 2014

⇨ The above information is reprinted with kind permission from *The Conversation*. Please visit www.theconversation.com for further information.

British firms top farm animal welfare approach table

Britain has topped a table rating food industry approaches to farm animal welfare reporting and management.

Egg supplier Noble Foods, retailers Marks & Spencer and Waitrose, and Swiss company the Coop Group attained the highest scores in the fourth annual Business Benchmark on Farm Animal Welfare (BBFAW) report.

Published today, the report assessed how 90 of the world's leading food companies, including 19 from the UK and 23 from the US, are managing and reporting their farm animal welfare policies and practices.

Each was given a percentage score, which took into account management commitment and policy, governance and management, innovation, and performance reporting. Based on their score, each company was ranked in one of six tiers.

Six of the 11 companies that made the two top tiers were British.

With a score of more than 80%, Marks & Spencer, Noble Foods, Waitrose and the Coop Group were placed in the top tier.

Alongside Unilever, McDonald's, Marfrig and Migros, with scores of between 62% and 80%, British retailers Cooperative Food and J Sainsbury and pork producer and processor Cranswick were deemed to have integrated such practices into their business strategies.

The 11 companies making up the top two tiers "have made strong commitments to farm animal welfare, have well-developed management systems and processes, and have a clear focus on farm animal welfare performance measures," said the report.

While a "consolidated and organised account for their approach to farm animal welfare" was offered by Tesco, it was deemed that there is "work to be done".

According to the report, 66% of the 90 companies assessed now have published farm animal welfare policies, compared to 46% in 2012.

Targets on farm animal welfare have also been published – 54%, up from 26% in 2012.

"The results show that it is realistic for companies across the world and in all sub-sectors (retailers, wholesalers, restaurants, bars and producers) to aspire to and achieve high scores in the Benchmark and to recognise the responsibility they hold for the welfare of animals in their supply chain," said Nicky Amos, executive director, BBFAW.

27 January 2016

⇨ The above information originally appeared in *Farmers Weekly* and is reprinted with kind permission. Please visit www.fwi.co.uk for further information.

The inhumane trade in European farm animals

By Olga Kikou

The European Union's animal welfare legislation is regarded as among the best in the world. But exported animals are no longer protected by EU transport or slaughter welfare laws once they leave its borders, writes Olga Kikou.

Olga Kikou is European Affairs Manager for Compassion in World Farming (CIWF), an international NGO working on the welfare of farm animals and sustainable farming and food.

During 2014, over two million farm animals were exported live from the EU to third countries in North Africa, the Middle East and Turkey. Exports of live animals are on the increase as the farming industry is in search of new markets.

However, serious welfare problems have tarnished this trade. A recent exhibition in the European Parliament called 'Live animal exports: the EU's cruellest trade', highlighted the suffering involved in long-distance live animal transport

and the inhumane slaughter that animals often face at journey's end.

The EU has put in place a number of legislative measures aiming to protect the welfare of animals. EU animal welfare legislation is regarded among the best in the world. However, conditions in third countries are vastly different from those in the EU and exported animals are no longer protected by EU transport or slaughter welfare laws once they leave its borders. In third countries, there is often no level of protection at all and slaughter practices are often in breach of the international standards of the World Organisation for Animal Health (OIE) on welfare of animals at slaughter.

A wide range of slaughter practices which cause great animal suffering are common in regions where EU animals end up. Investigations in a number of countries have shown animals slaughtered by cruel, unskilled and violent methods, causing severe pain and leaving them conscious and suffering for several minutes after any wounds are inflicted, until they eventually bleed to death.

Cattle are tethered to poles or trees and are forced to the ground, their leg tendons are sometimes severed to make them easier to control. Blunt knives are used to slash repeatedly at the animals' throats. Sheep are dragged by their rear legs, fleeces and horns, and are thrown onto their backs or sides for throat cutting. Cattle are beaten on the head with poles to force them to the ground.

In other cases, animals remain standing on all four legs while they slowly bleed from the neck. Often animals are killed at unofficial slaughter locations, dragged off trucks and chased down streets before they are slaughtered on the pavement, often outside butcher shops.

While many animals are sent to third countries for slaughter, others are sent to fattening farms first where they spend some time in filthy, cramped conditions before being sent for slaughter at a local abattoir or street-butcher. In their case, prolonging their lives might mean prolonging their suffering. Those sent for breeding could end up in systems that would be illegal in the EU and will still face inhumane slaughter at the end of their short lives. This is the end result of journeys that can last up to 14 days in cramped conditions, in trucks or ships, without proper rest, feed or water.

Despite overwhelming evidence of cruelty, the Commission will not discourage the export trade and member states continue to send animals abroad. Exports are on the rise and without any measures to ensure proper treatment of animals in third countries.

The EU even allows the export of animals to war zones where the authorities are completely unable to ensure proper slaughter conditions. In 2014, around one million animals were exported to Libya, a war-torn country. Animals are even exported to Syria. A most recent investigation found Hungarian and Romanian animals in Gaza.

There is an obvious irony here. Animals are regarded as sentient beings while in EU territory but the same animals are left to their fate once they're sent abroad. This is certainly a double standard that needs to be scrutinised and eliminated.

In fact, this trade in live animals is in breach of Article 13 TFEU which requires the EU and the member states to pay "full regard to the welfare requirements of animals" in formulating and implementing EU agriculture policy. The "full regard" condition has not been applied in the case of exports. Besides legal obligations, there are also welfare and ethical considerations surrounding the EU live animal trade which have not been addressed despite the fact that EU institutions have been informed many times in recent years of the very serious welfare problems experienced during transport and at slaughter by EU animals.

Why then does this trade exist and could any alternatives provide long-term solutions? The answer is that no trade can be associated with such serious mistreatment and abuse of animals; if it does exist, then it should be brought to an end and alternative solutions should be presented. Economic arguments should not push aside moral and ethical considerations. The EU has to prove that it is serious about its own rules and value system. It becomes imperative therefore for the EU to take responsibility for the welfare of its animals. Ending the exports of live animals is the only way to tackle such a clear-cut case of inhumane treatment.

Ending this trade does not actually mean economic hardship for farmers. On the contrary, replacing the trade in live animals with exports in meat is a viable alternative that presents economic opportunities for the agriculture sector. These opportunities provide the right incentive to make the replacement of live animal exports by meat products a priority for the EU and a long-term solution to a problem that has already tarnished the EU's image.

13 March 2015

⇨ The above information is reprinted with kind permission from EurActiv.com.

Activists protest at Manchester Airport over claim of greyhounds being transported to China

Protesters claim animals could be sold into illegal meat trade.

By Alexandra Rucki

Animal rights activists are staging a protest at Manchester Airport over claims 24 greyhounds are being transported to China.

The campaigners, from the group Caged North West, believe the dogs have been taken by ferry from Ireland to Manchester and will be flown abroad on Thursday evening.

The *Manchester Evening News* understands there are no scheduled cargo flights to China from Manchester on Thursday.

But the protesters are adamant the 24 greyhounds will be sent from Manchester to Germany, then to Macau in China to be used for greyhound racing or the meat trade.

According to a spokesman for the group, greyhounds in China are destroyed if they do not perform well.

In the early hours of Thursday morning the activists say they intercepted a Transit van at Lymm services in Cheshire carrying the greyhounds.

Footage has emerged of people apparently placing dogs in cargo boxes at night, although the location is not known.

The protesters have been waiting at the cargo entrance to Manchester Airport since before dawn on Thursday, but no Transit van carrying animals has yet been seen.

It is understood there are no scheduled cargo flights to China from Manchester on Thursday.

But Michael James, 35, co-founder of Caged North West said: "We received information 24 greyhounds are coming to Manchester from Ireland, they travelled on a ferry from Holyhead.

"We managed to intercept the vehicle at Lymm services. They are Manchester bound to Manchester Airport, the flight destination is China."

He added: "It is an emotive and major issue. Everyone we come across now, everyone is against it. Australia has banned greyhounds from travelling to China.

"In greyhound racing in China, if the dog does not place in the first three it will be destroyed. They are also sold into the illegal meat trade.

"If we can keep them in this country until 6.30pm they will be safe. We are not giving up, we are not leaving today."

As many as 40 protesters were said to be waiting at the airport overnight, but the number of participants has now scaled down to around seven.

A spokesman for Manchester Airport said: "This morning a small group of protesters held a peaceful demonstration on the airport site. This did not impact on operations in any way."

12 May 2016

⇨ The above information is reprinted with kind permission from the *Manchester Evening News*. Please visit www.manchestereveningnews.co.uk for further information.

China's Yulin dog meat festival – what we know

How many dogs are killed? Where do they come from? Is it true dogs are tortured first? Animals Asia's Cat and Dog Welfare team in China provides the answers.

1. How many dogs will die?

At its height the Yulin dog meat festival was said to be responsible for 10,000 to 15,000 slaughtered dogs. In 2014 that figure was reported as dropping to 2,000 to 3,000. Reliable sources last year put it at under 1,000.

2. How many dogs are eaten each year in China?

The widely reported – though difficult to verify - figure is ten million.

3. The festival is just about eating dogs?

The festival takes place to mark the summer solstice. This year that is 21 June. The festival's full name is the Yulin lychee and dog meat festival. There's also a lot of beer consumed. Sadly it has also been reported that cats are eaten too, though not in such vast numbers.

4. Can't the Government just stop it?

We believe we are reaching a point where there is little value for the Government in defending an industry that is being revealed as being more about crime than tradition. We'll ensure pressure continues to grow in the hope that the dog and cat meat eating industry is made illegal.

As far as the Yulin dog meat festival is concerned, it is no longer sanctioned on any level by government, so what you're seeing is a kind of unofficial agreement by dog meat lovers to meet up once a year.

It's why we say – yes we must end the Yulin dog meat festival – but to do that we must also end dog meat eating in China – and that's a year-round campaign.

5. But I heard the festival was cancelled?

This rumour goes around every year – usually due to confusion on social media regarding other festivals. We hope it does end but a gradually shrinking festival due to public pressure is more likely.

6. Where are the dogs sourced?

Our research shows that the idea that these dogs are 'farmed' is untrue. The vast majority are stolen, grabbed or poisoned or both and shoved into tiny cages with other dogs – they start a long journey to a dog meat trader. During this time they have no food or water and diseases spread quickly. These include canine distemper, parvovirus and, almost certainly, rabies.

7. Where do they go to?

Dog slaughterhouses are filthy, unregulated and cruel. No quarantine of the animals exists either at slaughter or during transport. These slaughterhouses are generally located far away from downtown areas and communities, but in places where eating dog and cat meat is more common, animals can be killed on the street.

8. How do they die?

This is a difficult question because there are no regulations on dog slaughtering. Typically they suffer a death that is far from efficient. They are snared around the neck with metal hooks and dragged from their cages. Then they are either bludgeoned or stabbed in the neck or groin to be 'bled out'. Other methods of killing including being hanged or electrocuted. This happens dog by dog so other dogs are likely to witness multiple deaths ahead of their own. This further spreads panic.

9. Is it true that dogs are 'boiled alive'?

While we don't believe this is a routine intention, inefficient slaughter techniques and the sheer scale of the killing involved means it's extremely probable that cooking of dogs can start before their death.

10. Is it true that dogs are beaten to improve the flavour of the meat?

This is an often-repeated accusation, and while there was some evidence of this many years ago, we are yet to find evidence of it occurring today. Our research suggests lingering deaths tend

to be as a result of an inefficient slaughter rather than a deliberate attempt to inflict pain.

11. Is it true that torturing of the dogs is part of the festival?

It's no exaggeration to say that what the dogs suffer is indeed 'torture'. However, we believe it's more likely that this torture is due to cruel catching, transportation and slaughter – rather than deliberate desire to prolong the pain of the dog for gratification, entertainment or to improve the dish in any way.

12. How common are dog and cat eating in China?

Although we know that the practice of eating cat and dog meat has existed for many years in China, especially in Guangdong, Guangxi, Guizhou province and north eastern China, the frequency of consumption and the amount consumed is decreasing year by year.

According to our *Survey of public attitudes to dog and cat eating in China* (released 2015), eating cat and dog meat is not universal nationwide. In cities outside those listed above, 20% of respondents

had eaten dog meat in the past two years, while in the same period, 1.7% had eaten cat meat.

Within the cities where dog meat eating is more favoured (including Guangdong, Guangxi, Guizhou province and north eastern China) almost half of respondents had not eaten cats or dogs in the past two years. Among those who had, half had eaten it only once or twice a year.

Thanks to all the effort (from NGOs to individuals, both domestic and overseas) put into improving animal welfare in China and their work with local authorities, the number of consumers of cat and dog meat keeps reducing every year.

13. Do people eat dog or cat due to lack of food or money?

No, despite many of the animals being stolen, the meat is still not cheap. It is eaten for reasons of superstition or tonic or, arguably, tradition. If it was made illegal tomorrow nobody would starve.

14. If Chinese people don't want the dog meat trade – then why don't they end it?

Influencing legislation is not easy, however, there have been significant

responses that will not have gone unnoticed. This includes close to nine million people voting online for proposed legislation to end cat and dog meat eating. Meanwhile – though dog theft stories are a constant in Chinese media – they still have the power to shock and there's a growing feeling that the time is now here for change.

The eating of cat and dog meat being made illegal would be widely welcomed and would cut crime and cruelty.

Grassroots NGOs and brave animal lovers are also responsible for numerous dog and cat rescues every year. This represents a huge undertaking because rescues start with stopping the truck but the care of the dogs or cats can go on for years afterwards.

15. What would happen to the dogs in Yulin if the festival was ended?

The most likely scenario is that increased year-on-year pressure will see the Yulin dog meat festival continue to reduce in size. Public pressure is already doing that and is very literally saving lives in the process. It is vital that this pressure is kept up. If there is no appetite for consumption then the supply will also dwindle – as will the cruelty. In the event that a festival was suddenly stopped we're confident that local groups – with our support – could rescue dogs.

There are many local rescue groups that have pushed for the end of the Yulin dog meat festival – with so many groups working so hard, we believe there would be no shortage in support for caring for the dogs and ultimately finding them new homes.

24 May 2016

⇨ The above information is reprinted with kind permission from Animals Asia. Please visit www.animalsasia.org for further information.

Why do people in China eat dog meat? %

A-class cities

- For taste
- Chinese tradition
- Because colleagues do
- Because my family does
- For health reasons
- To be sociable
- They are the same as livestock animals
- Unknown
- Aphrodisiac

A-class cities:
46.6
31.5
25.2
21.9
21.1
16.2
12.6
12.1
10.5

B-class cities
43.9
4.8
20.0
16.8
33.3
13.6
6.7
11.0
7.1

Source: Survey of public attitudes to dog and cat eating in China, Animals Asia, June 2015

A-class cities (where dog meat consumption is more common):
Yulin (Guangxi Zhuang Autonomous Region), Kaiping (Guangdong Province), Jinhua (Zhejiang Province), Yanji (Jilin Province), Harbin (Heilongjiang Province), Fushun (Liaoning Province)
B-class cities (where dog meat consumption is rare):
Beijing, Shanghai, Guangzhou (Guangdong Province), Shenzhen (Guangdong Province), Fuzhou (Fujian Province), Wuhan (Hubei Province), Chengdu (Sichuan Province), Zhengzhou (Henan Province), Xi'an (Shanxi Province), Baoding (Hebei Province), Jiujiang (Jiangxi Province), Dali (Yunnan Province), Baotou (Inner Mongolia Autonomous Region)

Charity reveals the shocking 'treats' fuelling the UK's pet obesity crisis

PDSA warns of pet obesity crisis fuelled by bad diets.

A combination of snacks, scraps, and takeaway leftovers continues to fuel an obesity crisis among our pets, according to leading vet charity, PDSA.

With new data showing that a staggering 5.5 million* cats, dogs and rabbits in the UK are being fed treats every day, the charity's vets are warning owners that they could be drastically shortening their pet's life expectancy.

Owners have admitted to indulging their pets by giving them fatty, sugary, and in some cases dangerous, foods. These include cake, chocolate, biscuits, crisps, chips, takeaway and even alcohol.

On top of all these unhealthy treats, over 4 million pets (2.6 million dogs, 1.4 million cats and 12,000 rabbits) are fed table scraps or leftovers as their main meals**. These diet disasters are taking their toll, according to PDSA, with a third of dogs and a quarter of cats now classed as overweight or obese***. Vet professionals predict that the problem will continue to grow – with 80% believing there will be more overweight pets than healthy ones by 2019****. Sadly, many overweight pets develop potentially life-threatening conditions such as heart disease, cancer and diabetes, as well as debilitating conditions including arthritis as a direct result of being overweight.

To help fight the flab PDSA launched its annual Pet Fit Club competition in February 2016 and invited owners of overweight and obese pets to take part in the UK's biggest and most successful pet slimming competition.

"Pet obesity can be tackled, and through a diet and exercise programme like Pet Fit Club we can transform fat pets into fit pets," said PDSA Vet Vicki Larkham-Jones.

Vicki continues: "Nearly half of pet owners believe that obesity is the biggest threat to animal welfare in the next ten years – yet pets continue to be fed unsuitable diets which is fuelling the problem.

"As well as being high in calories, food like takeaways, cake, cheese, chips and crisps are high in fat and sugars which are bad for our pets' waistlines and teeth. Some owners even admitted to giving chocolate and even alcohol, both of which are poisonous to pets and can be fatal.

"The good news is that we can make a real difference, starting now. With the right food and regular exercise, it is easy to keep pets fit and healthy. Over the past 11 years, PDSA Pet Fit Club has helped transform the lives of some of the UK's most obese pets. Through the competition we have helped over 100 animals lose more than 63 stone and encouraged thousands more owners to make positive changes to their pet's lifestyle. Once again we are inviting owners with overweight pets to enter."

About Pet Fit Club

Pet Fit Club is an annual six-month diet and exercise programme, tailored and overseen by expert PDSA vets and nurses. The charity select up to 12 overweight dogs, cats and rabbits from across the UK to participate each year.

PDSA Pet Fit Club was launched in 2005 and has already helped 74 dogs, 32 cats and 6 rabbits lose a total 63 stone 11lb - equivalent to over 400 bags of sugar, 6,500 tins of tuna, 7,000 sausages or four heavyweight boxers.

Pet obesity – the facts

⇨ Over 5.5 million pets – more than 3.3 million dogs, 2 million cats and 168,000 rabbits – are given daily treats*

⇨ Over 4 million UK pets (dogs, cats and rabbits) are fed scraps as their main meal**

⇨ Nearly 9 million owners give their pets treats because they believe it makes their furry friend feel happy*****

⇨ 88% of owners believe overweight pets have a shorter lifespan

⇨ 60% of owners think overweight pets are less happy

Pet treats – the facts

	Number of dogs	Number of cats	Number of rabbits
Alcohol	186,000	111,000	N/A
Chips	1,023,000	222,000	N/A
Crisps	1,116,000	666,000	48,000
Cake	83,7000	333,000	12,000
Human biscuits	2,232,000	222,000	84,000
Takeaway	651,000	333,000	N/A
Human chocolate	465,000	222,000	12,000

The number of pets fed unsuitable foods is fuelling the obesity crisis. High in sugar and fat, treats are bad for their teeth as well as their waistlines. Some of the treats owners admitting giving, including chocolate and alcohol are poisonous and can prove fatal:

Pet Fit Club participants will receive free diet pet food for the duration of the competition, courtesy of Dechra. The overall Pet Fit Club Champ, who will be crowned at the end of 2016, will win a year's free diet food and a pet friendly holiday courtesy of cottages.com.

Case studies

Cilla and Shyla

American Bulldogs, Cilla and Shyla, from Liverpool, who need to lose over four stone (28kg) between them, have been put on a diet.

Curvy Cilla, who is thought to be named after one of the city's most famous stars - the late singer Cilla Black - weighs in at over 9 stone (58kg), while her canine companion Shyla tips the scales slightly lower, but still hefty, 7 stone 9lbs (50kg).

Their owners, the Thomas family from Anfield, admit having fed Cilla (8) and Shyla (5) too many treats in the past but that has all changed over the past few weeks following advice from PDSA vets.

Alan Thomas (49) said they regularly gave the portly pooches treats including crumpets, pasta, and biscuits. Dog biscuits were given 'like they were going out of fashion'.

He said: "We adopted Cilla from an animal rescue centre in Liverpool and they gave her the name. She was actually very underweight when we first brought her home. We spoilt her because she'd had such a rotten start to life after being abandoned.

"She's had to have a few operations on her eyes and ears and for a while she was taking medication which increased her appetite. To make matters worse she wouldn't eat the

tablets unless they were hidden in a crumpet!

"With Shyla, her weight gain is more down to us. We just can't resist her puppy dog eyes or begging. She's a very intelligent dog and loves to watch TV. Horse racing is her favourite – she sits glued to the screen until they finish when she lies down."

Alan said the family are now thinking about portion control when feeding the dogs and have stopped dishing out treats.

Zorro

Zorro the cat had piled on the pounds, much like his animated counterpart Puss-in-Boots in the Shrek movies. He used to spend his days lazing around sneaking his favourite cheese and onion crisps. But his owner noticed he was so fat he was struggling to clean himself properly, so she decided it was time to put this ginger puss into Boot Camp! Despite his continued begging for food, Zorro swash buckled his way to losing a fifth of his bodyweight, and was the cat winner of Pet Fit Club in 2014!

Merlin

When biscuit-loving Merlin joined Pet Fit Club in 2012, he weighed a whopping 42.2kg, making him 111% above his ideal weight. This obese Border Collie lost 20cm off

his waistline, making him a much healthier and happier dog!

Tia

Larger-than-life Tia used to love playing in the local reservoir, but the lazy Lab lost her way and opted to snooze rather than swim. When she joined Pet Fit Club in 2013, she weighed almost double what she should. Tia slimmed down by 4.2kg during the competition, losing 10cm from her waistline.

Casper

This mega moggy was rescued as a kitten in a very sorry state – infested with fleas and very underweight. Following his rescue he developed a massive appetite and would steal food at any opportunity. He ballooned to 8.6kg (91% over his ideal weight), but during the competition in 2012 he managed to shed the pounds meaning he was much more active and loved playing with his feline friend once more.

Based on estimated populations of 9.3 million dogs, 11.1 million cats and 1.2 million rabbits:

*36% of dogs, 18% of cats and 14% of rabbits receive treats on a daily basis. (9,300,000 x 36/100 = 3,348,000; 11,100,000 X 18/100 = 1,998,000; 1,200,000 X14/100 = 168,000)

**28% of dogs, 13% of cats and 1% of rabbits are fed table scraps or leftovers as part their main meal.

*** Data sourced from PDSA's nationwide PetCheck tour

**** The survey was carried out face-to-face to a sample of 1,127 veterinary professionals, including vets, vet nurses, veterinary care assistants, and vet and veterinary nursing students. Figures are not weighted. In addition, a survey was carried out online through an open link. Fieldwork was undertaken between 18 September and 10 October 2014. Total sample size was 572 veterinary professionals.

80% of veterinary professionals believe there will be more overweight pets than healthy weight pets in the five years' time.

*****39% of dogs, 43% of cats and 36% of rabbit owners surveyed give their pets treats because they believe it makes them feel happy.

2015

⇨ The above information is reprinted with kind permission from the PDSA. Please visit www.pdsa.org.uk for further information.

"Breed-specific legislation: a dog's dinner" says RSPCA after Hank is spared death

Breed-specific dog legislation – the law which saw Belfast dog Hank snatched from his owners and put on death row – is unnecessary and hundreds of pets have been put down needlessly, the RSPCA have warned.

The animal charity has called for a change in the law which regularly sees animals put down because of their breed.

The Dangerous Dogs Act forces police and many animal rescue organisations to put dogs down because of the way they look rather than the danger they pose, the RSPCA says.

The law – which banned the pit bull terrier, Japanese Tosa, Dogo Argentino and Fila Brasileiro breeds based on their physical appearance - was introduced 25 years ago last month.

Recently, Hank was taken from his home in east Belfast and held by Belfast City Council while an expert assessed his breed.

While he was found to be a pit bull terrier, his good nature meant he was deemed to "not pose a risk to the public".

In the past two years the RSPCA said it had been "forced" to put 366 dogs down under section one of the Act, which covers breed-specific offences.

Launching its report *Breed Specific Legislation: A Dog's Dinner*, the charity called on the Government to probe the effectiveness of section one, urging it to be repealed completely.

RSPCA dog welfare expert Dr Samantha Gaines said: "The police, the RSPCA and other animal rescue organisations have to deal with the consequences of this flawed law by euthanising hundreds of dogs because legislation is forcing us to due to the way they look, despite being suitable for rehoming.

"Not only is this a huge ethical and welfare issue, it also places significant emotional strain on staff."

The RSPCA said there was not enough evidence to show that such legislation reduced dog bites and called into question the evidence required to classify a dog as being of a prohibited type.

Dr Gaines added: "The RSPCA believes it is paramount for the Government to launch an inquiry into the effectiveness of BSL (breed-specific legislation), assess other options to improve human safety and dog welfare, and ultimately repeal the breed-specific part of the legislation."

Dog behaviour expert Victoria Stilwell threw her weight behind the campaign, condemning the legislation.

She said: "BSL tears apart families while punishing innocent dogs and their guardians solely because of a dog's appearance. Any dog can bite under the right circumstances, so legislation should focus on protecting the public through responsible pet guardianship rather than targeting a particular breed."

Last month Battersea Dogs and Cats Home released a report calling on the Government to review the Dangerous Dogs Act, saying current legislation is "flawed" and instead should target irresponsible owners.

9 August 2016

⇨ The above information is reprinted with kind permission from the *Belfast Telegraph*. Please visit www.belfasttelegraph.co.uk for further information.

In defence of the petting zoo

By Michael Oliver

You may hear people over the next day or so bleating (pun definitely intended) about how immoral and cruel the petting zoo is. The fact of the matter is, however, that this sort of event is beneficial to all parties concerned, even including the animals.

Animals used for these sort of events are, by their very nature, sociable creatures. Positive interaction such as that seen today can only be beneficial to these domesticated creatures. From the animal's perspective, although having 1,500 ugly mutts staring at you in a gormless manner expelling strange noises in your direction will surely seem like a chore after a while, it surely beats yet another day in the field looking at the same patch of sky or ceiling having (probably) nothing to do all day, although if you believe the naysayers (or should that be neighsayers?) then they MUST hate it because they all love standing around in a field somewhere in their 'natural habitat'. Boredom is a big problem for domesticated animals, and they are cleverer than they look; positive activity and intriguing new surroundings (still with familiar people) will provide stimulation which can only serve to provide some respite to their mundane lives (although being a dog would be the coolest thing ever). Animals love attention – it's far better for them to be given some than be ignored in a random field, pen or room somewhere.

So the animals probably had a good time, and there was very little danger of them feeling distressed, with expert staff on hand to ensure things ran smoothly, yet were still familiar to the animals. If any of them were showing signs of distress then there was the facility to take them out of the pen. Hay and straw was provided, so there should be no animal welfare issues whatsoever.

Judging by the number of snapchats I received, people seemed to be enjoying the event, and it's a great way to ensure that many students have a small glimmer of respite from their otherwise dreary, caffeine-filled January. The whole purpose of the event was to 'de-stress', and if people came away from the redbrick feeling happy then what's the problem?

13 January 2016

⇨ The above information is reprinted with kind permission from Wessex Scene. Please visit www.wessexscene.co.uk for further information.

Climbing the tree: the case for chimpanzee 'personhood'

***This article is from* The Conversation.**

THE CONVERSATION

By Jane Johnson, Research Officer, Macquarie University

Hercules and Leo don't know it, but a decision about their future has made history. In granting an order to show cause on whether Hercules and Leo (who just happen to be chimpanzees) are illegally imprisoned, a Supreme Court judge in Manhattan has kept open the possibility that some nonhuman animals will be granted legal rights under common law.

The plaintiffs are currently used for biomedical research at New York's Stony Brook University. What the lawyers running the case hope to show is that Hercules and Leo shouldn't be treated as if they were just things or property, but should instead be given the status of persons.

Showing that any animal has what is needed for legal personhood is a difficult task. But chimpanzees seem promising candidates as there is a wealth of scientific evidence showing they possess complex cognitive abilities, like self-awareness and autonomy.

The order to show cause on the issue of habeas corpus is the first step in a process which Steven Wise and the Nonhuman Rights Project (NhRP) hope will secure Hercules and Leo's bodily liberty and integrity.

If the court were to find in their favour, the chimpanzees would no longer be kept for research and could be moved to a sanctuary in Florida.

NhRP was founded by Wise in 2007 and after years of research it filed its first cases back in December 2013. To date it has brought three cases on behalf of chimpanzees held in captivity in the state of New York. But NhRP is ambitious, aiming to run as many cases on behalf of animals as it can fund.

If it can find suitable plaintiffs, NhPR hopes to mount cases for the personhood of elephants, whales and dolphins too.

Different perspectives on personhood for animals

Reactions to treating nonhuman animals as persons vary widely. Some people think it is ridiculous

to even entertain the idea. Persons have to be human – end of story.

For philosophers, this is not very satisfactory. It tries to answer the question of whether animals can be persons by asserting a definition rather than offering an argument. It gets more interesting when people give reasons to support their view.

One approach to defending the idea that only humans are persons involves saying that persons need to participate in society. Society is founded on reciprocity; you can't just take rights without also assuming responsibilities. And animals like chimpanzees can't take on responsibilities, so they can't have rights.

Another tactic is to suggest that there is a whole heap of criteria that one has to meet to be a person. And although humans meet these criteria, nonhuman animals don't. These criteria could include things like being rational, self-aware, autonomous, having culture and being able to communicate.

The problem is neither of these kinds of arguments stand up to interrogation. There are lots of humans who get the benefit of rights without living up to reciprocal responsibilities, such as young children and people with certain physical or mental impairments.

There are similar difficulties when using a criteria-based approach. Just as there are many humans who don't meet certain criteria for personhood, there are some nonhuman animals who do.

This is known as the 'problem of marginal cases'. Taking a consistent approach would mean treating some animals, but not all humans, as worthy of moral consideration.

There are other people who are sympathetic towards giving greater ethical consideration to animals, but who don't think using personhood is the best approach. Utilitarians, for example, worry about the capacity to suffer. If a chimpanzee – or for that matter a dog, cat or rat – can experience pleasure and pain, then they matter regardless of whether they meet a test for personhood.

Implications of nonhuman animals as persons

If Wise and the NhRP win their case it will be a significant precedent and other cases will surely follow. Chimpanzees in jurisdictions where successful cases are mounted will no longer be permitted to be used in research or kept in zoos and circuses.

However, less charismatic animals – ones that don't look like us or where it is not in our interests to grant them rights – won't be so fortunate. Historically,

there is a deep inconsistency in how we treat different types of animals that is not easily overturned, even in the face of compelling legal and ethical arguments.

The case of Hercules and Leo also has connections to Australia. Wise was inspired to practise animal law back in the 1980s after reading the work of Australian philosopher, Peter Singer. The hearing of the case in New York was actually interrupted due to Wise's long-standing commitment to visit Australia and deliver the 2015 Voiceless Animal Law Lecture Series.

The hearing is now scheduled for 10:30am Wednesday 27 May at the New York County Supreme Court. Those interested in seeking rights for nonhuman animals keenly await the outcome.

19 May 2015

⇨ The above information is reprinted with kind permission from *The Conversation*. Please visit www.theconversation.com for further information.

Gorilla's death calls for human responsibility, not animal personhood

This article is from The Conversation.

THE CONVERSATION

By Richard L. Cupp, John W. Wade Professor of Law, Pepperdine University

My reaction to the killing of Harambe the gorilla at the Cincinnati Zoo when a child went into the gorilla's enclosure is probably typical: I am sickened and I am angry. This must not happen again.

One step that some advocates will surely press for in light of Harambe's killing is to change our legal system to designate gorillas and other great apes such as chimpanzees as legal persons.

Expanding legal personhood to include intelligent nonhuman animals would give them legal rights, and would create standing for a human guardian to initiate legal actions on their behalf – much like children's rights are protected in courts by guardians.

At first blush this may sound progressive and enlightened, but in reality the concept is fundamentally flawed and dangerous for society.

Turning to our legal system in responding to Harambe's tragedy is the right approach, but our legal focus should be on ensuring effective human responsibility for the proper treatment of gorillas and other nonhuman animals rather than on pretending that gorillas are people.

Protections for animals

At surface, legal personhood for intelligent nonhuman animals has an edgy appeal and is often compared by its advocates to the noble battles to attain civil rights for marginalised humans.

Illustrating growing popular interest in the concept, a documentary about the legal battle for nonhuman animal personhood entitled *Unlocking the Cage* made its debut in January at the Sundance Film Festival. It is now opening in some cinemas, and will be aired on HBO, BBC and other television outlets later this year. The documentary highlights lawsuits filed in New York seeking to have intelligent chimpanzees treated as legal persons so that the chimpanzees would be removed from confined environments and placed in less restrictive, more natural environments.

These lawsuits do not seek to set the captive chimpanzees loose on the streets, but rather seek to have them moved to chimpanzee sanctuaries. Their arguments are based primarily on chimpanzees' impressive cognitive abilities, asserting that as "self-aware, autonomous beings" they are "entitled to such basic legal rights as bodily liberty and integrity". Significantly, the organisation behind the lawsuits has indicated that it also plans to pursue legal personhood for other great apes (which include gorillas), as well as elephants and dolphins.

Would Harambe's tragic killing have been avoided if our legal system considered a gorilla to be a legal person? Probably. A zoo likely would not be permitted to confine a legal person for viewing by the public. But although the nonhuman animal personhood approach has dramatic flair, it is not needed to change our laws regarding great apes and zoos.

Whether animals with the intelligence of great apes should be kept in any zoos, even high-quality zoos, is an increasingly serious question appropriate for thoughtful deliberation. And if the argument that they should not carries the day, this can be readily accomplished by changing the laws within our existing legal framework.

In other words, we do not need to pretend that great apes are people to protect them. Engaging in this pretension would be, in my view, both illogical and dangerous.

Society is rapidly evolving to demand greater protections for nonhuman animals, and appropriately so. Maintaining the status quo regarding levels of protection is in many instances neither feasible nor desirable.

But we are also increasingly facing a question with weighty societal

implications. Will we channel this evolution through the animal welfare paradigm of enhanced human responsibility toward nonhuman animals? Or will we channel it through the radical paradigm of legal personhood and human-like rights for nonhuman animals?

In our society, legal personhood is anchored in the human community's expectations of reciprocity from moral agents. We recognise that humans have rights, but we also generally expect them to accept responsibilities that come with belonging to or interacting with our society. Extending personhood beyond humans and their proxies would be inconsistent with our society's core foundational principles.

When an adult chimpanzee at the Los Angeles Zoo mauled a baby chimpanzee to death in front of zoo visitors in 2012, of course officials did not consider putting the chimpanzee on trial for murder. Although chimpanzees are highly intelligent as compared to most nonhuman animals, none of them are capable enough to be held morally responsible under our society's laws. We should not dilute the protections and responsibilities connected to personhood by extending it to nonhumans incapable of the level of accountability we generally impose on humans.

Cognitive test?

Corporate personhood – the granting of legal standing and some legal rights to corporations – does not negate humanity's centrality to personhood, because corporate personhood was created merely as a proxy for the rights and responsibilities of the humans who own the corporation. Regardless of whether corporate personhood is good or bad or whether it has been extended too far in recent Supreme Court cases, it is undeniably intended as a tool for representing human interests.

Further, analysing courts' and advocates' rationales for assigning legal personhood and rights to humans who lack significant moral agency, such as young children and humans with significant cognitive impairments, demonstrates that their belonging in the human community, rather than an assessment of their cognitive abilities, is the anchor of their rights and legal personhood. I have published separate law review articles addressing in much more detail why the legal personhood of young children and the legal personhood of humans with significant cognitive impairments do not support legal personhood for intelligent nonhuman animals.

Humans are the only beings that we know of where the norm is capacity to shoulder the mutual obligations that are at a foundational level related to legal rights in our society. Among other beings of which we are aware, not only do no other types of animals meet this norm, no individual members of any other types of animals meet this norm.

The most vulnerable humans, those with significant cognitive limitations, would face the greatest risks in a shift to considering individual cognitive capacities as a basis for legal personhood. Although the legal personhood paradigm we assign to them would not immediately collapse, over time thinking of personhood in terms of individual abilities could erode their protections.

Nonhuman animal legal personhood presents other intractable problems, such as articulating a workable approach to determining how far down the intelligence chain personhood should extend.

Every species of mammals and many other nonhuman animals demonstrate some level of autonomy, indeed probably more autonomy than some humans with particularly severe cognitive limitations, such as, for example, humans in a persistent vegetative state. To ensure 'equality,' should all of these animals be designated as legal persons?

More legal cases to come

Fortunately, New York's courts have unanimously rejected nonhuman animal legal personhood thus far. By my count at least 23 New York judges have participated in ruling against the cases at various stages of the litigation. In the most prominent appellate opinion to date the court dismissed one of the lawsuits by focusing on chimpanzees' incapacity to bear the societal responsibilities that are at a foundational level associated with rights.

But we are just at the beginning of what will be a long-term struggle. Many more lawsuits will likely be filed over the years in many jurisdictions. The ultimate outcome is far from clear, and the stakes are high.

Concluding that intelligent nonhuman animals such as Harambe should not be legal persons does not excuse us from doing more to protect them. Harambe's outrageous death provides a powerful illustration. The facts surrounding his death must be extensively investigated to determine whether the zoo, the child's parents, or any other humans or human proxies should be held legally accountable.

Regardless of whether the zoo's employees made the right decision in shooting Harambe, wrong decisions must have been made earlier that allowed this tragedy to take place.

If no laws or regulations were violated, the laws and regulations almost certainly need to be changed to ensure that this does not happen again. But our focus needs to be on demanding appropriate responsibility from morally accountable humans and human institutions, rather than on the dangerous pretence of nonhuman animal personhood.

3 June 2016

⇨ The above information is reprinted with kind permission from *The Conversation*. Please visit www.theconversation.com for further information.

Political animals 2015

Public baffled by delays on wild animal circus ban

More than three years after the Government committed to ending the use of wild animals in circuses, legislation to prohibit what the Prime Minister called an "outdated practice" has still to be introduced, despite that an implementation deadline of 1 December 2015 had been set for The Wild Animals in Circuses Bill, published in 2013.

There are very few issues that unite Parliament and public such as this – across all parties 94% of MPs stood for election on manifesto commitments to end wild animal circuses. The Conservative manifesto promised "we will ban wild animals in circuses". Public support for a ban on wild animals in circuses has remained consistently high for over a decade, evidenced in opinion polls commissioned by ADI. A 2010 Defra public consultation recorded:

⇨ 94.5% believed a ban on the use of wild animals in travelling circuses was the best option to achieve consistently better welfare standards for these animals.

⇨ 95.5% believed that there are no species of wild animal, for which it is acceptable to use in travelling circuses.

⇨ 96% believed travelling circuses should be prevented from obtaining any further wild animals.

Prior to the last General Election, the Government's own Bill was introduced as a Private Members' Bill by Jim Fitzpatrick MP 12 times and blocked each time by a handful of Conservative backbenchers. Clearly the longpromised government action is the only way forward.

The legislation applies only to England; Wales is committed to a ban and is seeking to be included in the legislation – although the Welsh Conservatives commented in September: "Whilst the Welsh Labour Government has said that it is supportive of a ban, for some reason they seem reluctant to tackle the issue head on and have instead deferred it to the UK Government to take decisive action."

In Scotland, following a public consultation where 98% favoured a ban on wild animal performances, Scotland's Rural Affairs Secretary Richard Lochhead announced he was "considering the best way forward and will set out our plans shortly".

All of which makes the political inertia baffling and disappointing to the public

An end to wild animals in circuses is a popular measure that will protect animals and bring the UK into line with over 30 countries which have already introduced similar animal protection measures. The delay in passing the legislation has already seen the return of a lion and tiger act to Britain's shores – which has now set up in Wales where temporary regulations – introduced in 2013 as a prelude to the ban – do not apply. The show has been criticised on both public safety and welfare grounds and ADI has documented the animals exhibiting abnormal, repetitive behaviours described by vet Marc Abraham as "a sure sign their welfare is severely compromised". Wildlife vet Simon Adams describes the living space for the animals – cages on the back of a truck with restricted access to a small exercise area – "unsuitable to big cats".

The evidence supporting a ban on the use of wild animals in circuses is overwhelming. Travelling circuses cannot hope to replicate a wild animal's natural habitat, or create a complex environment where its natural behavioural repertoire can be satisfied. In circumstances of constant travel, with most of the year spent in temporary, collapsible accommodation, it is inevitable that welfare will be compromised. In addition, these are powerful wild animals whose very nature has not been modified by thousands of years of human intervention, unlike domesticated species such as horses and dogs. As a result, apart from the tricks they are forced to perform, even the day-to-day care of these animals requires a very high level of control and subjugation, resulting in workers using violence due to fear, or time pressures.

ADI has conducted undercover investigations inside circuses all over the world, and each time our field officers have been able to actually work behind the scenes, inside the industry, we have filmed systematic violence and abuse of the animals, particularly during training or rehearsals. Some of the worst violence towards circus animals recorded by ADI has been behind the scenes in British circuses.

This evidence has led to successful cruelty convictions and a decade of public support for a ban, as the popularity of animal circuses has plunged. 20 years ago, 20 circuses toured the UK with 291 wild animals. Today, two circuses plus the lion and tiger act currently appearing in Wales, amounts to 24 wild animals. There is no economic rationale for allowing this cruel and out-dated practice to continue.

200 local authorities in the UK have banned either all, or wild animal acts, from council-owned land. Over 30 countries have introduced national bans across Europe, Latin America and Asia. The claim that a ban might be overturned following legal challenge in Europe proved groundless as the challenge to Austria's ban was defeated. ADI is currently in Peru assisting their government enforce a ban on wild animals in circuses, an operation that has seen ADI and Peruvian officials raid circuses all over the country, rescuing 24 lions, a tiger, a puma, monkeys and other animals. ADI previously undertook a similar operation in Bolivia.

As a nation which prides itself on being a champion of animal protection, it is time for England, Scotland and Wales to act. The Wild Animals in Circuses Bill has gathered dust for too long, it is time to keep the promise made to the public and outlaw this relic of the past, from a time when little was understood of the intelligence, communication and complex social and environmental needs of other species.

Death of Cecil reveals worldwide desire for greater wildlife protection

In July, the global outrage following the killing of Cecil the lion and the revelations about the world of trophy hunting was a very clear expression of the public's abhorrence over the killing of beautiful and iconic wild animals, as well as the impact that this cruel pastime has on threatened wildlife populations.

Lions are reportedly already extinct in 25 African countries and close to extinction in ten others, with numbers across the continent estimated at just 15,000 – 20,000 compared to around 200,000 in the 1980s. According to the IUCN, "there is not a population of lions in West or Central Africa that is large enough to be viable" and it is thought that in 10–20 years, the lion could disappear from the wild altogether.

Urgent action is needed to protect this majestic species, and other wild animals under threat. ADI is calling for the import of hunting trophies to be banned in the UK and across Europe. This measure has also been proposed in the US (the world's largest importer), where several bills to ban hunting trophy imports and curtail the wider wildlife trade have also been introduced.

A hunting trophy ban would be good news for conservation and makes good economic sense for African communities looking to find ways to conserve and benefit from their wildlife. Contrary to claims by the minority of hunters, trophy hunting contributes very little to local communities. It is wider tourism that provides income to greater numbers in local communities. A 2013 economic report concludes "hunting companies contribute only 3% of their revenue to communities living in hunting areas". And, that the trophy hunting industry "is tiny, contributing at best a fraction of a per cent of GDP. Nature-based tourism does play a significant role in national development, but trophy hunting is insignificant. Across the investigated countries, trophy hunting revenue was only 1.8% of tourism revenues."

It is felt that trophy hunting also encourages poaching, due to other parts of the animals feeding into the illicit trade for animal parts. More must also be done to protect elephants from poaching, 30,000 elephants have lost their lives in the last few years alone.

Despite the introduction of a number of measures to clamp down on the illegal trade, the latest figures by the CITES programme for Monitoring the Illegal Killing of Elephants show that poaching rates remain largely unchanged. If this relentless slaughter is to be effectively tackled, the trade in legal ivory must stop. ADI calls for an EU-wide ban on the import, export and sale of ivory as well as a ban on the import of wild elephants captured for zoo collections, such as the round-ups that have taken place in the same national park in Zimbabwe from which Cecil was lured.

The reaction to the killing of Cecil showed how trophy hunters are completely at odds with the views of the majority on the protection of wildlife – and when these animals are apparently up for grabs for the highest bidder to shoot for fun, it is much more difficult to raise the general level of respect for other species and persuade communities to value and protect their wildlife for future generations.

Hunting Act protects animals

The Hunting Act, as it stands, prohibits hunts across England and Wales from using a pack of dogs to flush out and chase a wild animal across the countryside to the point of exhaustion and ultimately to its death. It is the most successful legislation of its kind, enjoying overwhelming public support and with 378 convictions since it was introduced. Latest figures show 80% of the public back a ban on fox hunting, 86% a ban on deer hunting and 88% a ban on hare hunting and 'coursing'.

A free vote on the repeal of the legislation was promised by the Conservative Party in its election manifesto; however, plans to amend the Hunting Act through a statutory instrument were unexpectedly announced in July – however, the vote was cancelled following increasing opposition.

ADI considers it imperative to retain the Hunting Act in its present form and we urge MPs to oppose measures to repeal this important wildlife legislation. The use of hunting with hounds for 'wildlife management' is considered inefficient and inhumane, with studies showing that not only are fox populations unaffected by hunting but their predation of farmed animals has a minimal impact.

Badger cull in England

ADI joins eminent experts, veterinarians, MPs and the public in opposing the badger cull on scientific, as well as economic and welfare grounds. With the pilot culls in Gloucestershire, Somerset and now Dorset underway, the Government is pursuing the policy and setting aside the scientific and economic arguments against this poorly conceived scheme. ADI is calling for a review of the bovine TB control strategy and a move away from the ineffective, inhumane killing of wildlife towards more frequent testing, stringent disease controls and vaccination.

Badger cull facts

⇨ The pilot culls are carried out over four years, for six-week periods

⇨ Somerset and Gloucestershire have entered into their third year, with Dorset in its first year

⇨ The aim is to reduce the local badger population by at least 70%

⇨ Three out of four of culls to date have fallen well short of the minimum target, with a low of less than 40%

⇨ 2,476 badgers have been killed (2013/4)

⇨ £16.7 million has been spent (2012–4) – £6,775 per badger

⇨ The success of more frequent testing of cattle herds has been demonstrated in other parts of Britain: Scotland has been declared TB free since 2009 following more frequent tests of high-risk herds; Wales has had annual or more frequent testing in place since January 2010 for ALL herds, with a 23% reduction in incidents announced last year. However, England continues to conduct less frequent testing – every four years – except in areas where there is a high incidence of TB, where annual testing is carried out.

Three reasons why the cull must stop

1. A scientific study published in 2007 after the Randomised Badger Culling Trial, which was conducted over nine years, concluded: "badger culling cannot meaningfully contribute to the future control of cattle TB in Britain".

2. An independent expert panel commissioned by the Government last year found that the badger culls were ineffective. The panel also noted that up to 18% of badgers killed took longer than five minutes to die, over three times the 5% standard set by the Government.

3. "The main conclusion" of an analysis of government TB statistics published in September 2015: "more frequent testing is leading to lower TB infections in cattle both in terms of TB prevalence as well as TB incidence." Co-

author Professor Matthew Evans, of Queen Mary University of London concluded "It is clear that testing cattle frequently is the most effective way of reducing bovine TB."

Primates as pets

Primates are not suitable pets. The welfare of primate pets is severely compromised and poorly protected by legislation. ADI believes that a ban on the keeping of monkeys and lesser apes is the only way to ensure these emotional, intelligent animals do not suffer through ignorance and poor environments.

Primates have not been bred for domestic traits over thousands of years; they are highly social and have evolved to live in an extensive, rich environment in the wild, nurtured by the company of their own species and stimulated by a challenging habitat. A life of captivity – and, for many, confinement and isolation – leads to frustration and psychological problems, resulting in stereotypic, repetitive behaviours which can include self-mutilation, pacing and teeth-grinding.

The lack of protection for these animals is illustrated by the fact that no official numbers are kept on primate pets in the UK, with estimates varying widely from 900 to more than 7,500 individuals. There is no information on the source of these animals.

An inquiry into the keeping of primates as pets in the UK was launched by the Environment, Food and Rural Affairs Committee (EFRA) in December 2013. In a written submission, ADI recommended that the UK Government take immediate action to end the import and sale of primates for the pet trade, in light of the inevitable suffering involved in the capture, transport and social isolation of these animals, the damage caused to wild populations by the trade and the risk to human health from unknown monkey viruses.

ADI also recommended the national licensing of all species of

privately-owned primates, which would set standards of welfare and environmental enrichment and make provision for the removal of animals kept in unsuitable conditions.

The EFRA report, published in June 2014 made six key recommendations, stopping short of calling for a primate pet ban. The Government published what ADI considered to be an extremely disappointing response – although Defra has stated that primates should not be kept as pets, limited action has been proposed to tackle this issue. ADI continues to urge the Government to stop the keeping of primate pets as these animals currently endure inadequate and inappropriate conditions.

It is worth noting that in Peru, whilst enforcing the ban on wild animals in circuses, ADI is assisting the Government with a drive to end the keeping of primates as pets. The country has a major problem with some 35 indigenous species of primates taken from forests and streaming into the illegal wildlife trade, especially infants captured after parents are killed for bushmeat. The Government of Peru has launched an awareness campaign with the simple message "Your house is not my home" (Tu Casa No Es Mi Hogar) and in addition to seizures of monkeys from restaurants and private owners, ADI is supporting this with educational displays at airports.

We hope the British Government can set a positive example with the message that houses on the other side of the world from the natural habitat of these primates, is most certainly NOT a suitable home.

⇨ The above information is reprinted with kind permission from Animal Defenders International. Please visit www.ad-international.org for further information.

Don't be fooled into elephant abuse

By Dave Neale, Animal Welfare Director

To be in the presence of an elephant is an amazing experience. Their sheer size overwhelms you, and their gentle social nature leaves you with a sense of calm and fulfilment that life can be and should be friendly and peaceful.

Yet this calm, good-natured temperament is repeatedly exploited.

Most recently, images of young western tourists in Thailand riding baby elephants through drunken pool parties rightly shocked many. But it should also serve as a reminder how easily people can be made ignorant of serious animal welfare issues.

To the enormous detriment of one of nature's most awe-inspiring animals, we have learnt that if we physically and psychologically abuse these gentle giants we can force them into situations which we convince ourselves are amusing and entertaining.

The myriad elephant riding opportunities for travellers visiting Southeast Asian destinations are a prime example. What could be more 'natural' than spending a few hours in the company of an elephant, exercising and washing them? After all, in many cases these elephants have been 'rescued' from a life of hard labour on logging camps.

But often all is not as it seems.

Throughout your elephant riding experience, you will be in the 'caring' hands of a mahout, a person that understands their elephant like no other. Yet in most cases this person will be in possession of an instrument to ensure your elephant remains under control. To provide such close contact experiences with such a powerful animal brings inevitable safety issues.

To mitigate the risks and protect your safety, the mahout will use a sharpened tool or hook to 'guide' your elephant into the places and positions that you desire. The bullhook or similar tool is also used in some situations to mete out physical punishment. No matter how gently the bullhook may be used with an animal in your presence, at some point it first had to be established as a negative reinforcer. That means causing enough pain and discomfort for the animal to remember and seeks to avoid that pain by complying with instructions. A smaller handheld 'jab-stick' may also be used to stab the elephant in sensitive places such as behind the ears, to ensure it complies as desired for the tourist.

The use of these instruments removes an elephant's choice and control over its immediate environment and actions. The majestic animal is forced to comply with the wishes of the trainer regardless of whether or not the action is in its best interests.

Elsewhere, elephants are also forced to endure the indignity and physical pain of performing circus tricks for entertainment. Elephants standing on their heads or spinning in circles only confirms our role as manipulators of all things beautiful. The animals themselves endure pain and indignity time after time to prevent them from receiving further physical punishments.

When you stop to consider all this from the elephant's point of view, suddenly it does not seem quite so fun or innocent.

For many of these elephants, they started their lives in the wild with their family herds, only to be ripped away by human hands, beaten into submission via a brutal training regime, and forced into a life of abject misery on a logging or a tourist camp. Others have had the misfortune of being born into this life, subjected to abuse from the moment they were born.

If you truly love and respect elephants, do not ride them, do not pose for your photograph with them, and do not pay to see them perform circus tricks.

There are places which have truly rescued elephants from lives of misery, places that allow elephants to be elephants in the company of peers and do not force them to perform tricks or provide rides and 'close contact experiences'. These are the places that provide true sanctuary.

Credible sanctuaries can be recognised by the following aspects:

⇨ the elephants live in groups, and are not subjected to isolated confinement

⇨ the elephants are not chained

⇨ violence is not used in interactions with the elephants

⇨ no breeding takes place at the facility

⇨ there is no contact between tourists and the elephants.

One such place is the Elephant Transit Home in Udawalawe, Sri Lanka. The orphaned elephants here can generally only be seen at feeding times, when they can be watched from a viewing platform for about 20 minutes while they are given milk. The rest of the time they spend in the National Park, out of view of people, in preparation for their return to the wild. Here, the elephants' welfare comes first – as it should at all true sanctuaries.

24 April 2015

⇨ The above information is reprinted with kind permission from Animals Asia. Please visit www.animalsasia.org for further information.

It is time to see through the marketing tactics of the European fur industry

By Salla Tuomivaara and Siri Martinsen

Member states have an opportunity to play a leading role for animal welfare globally by phasing out fur farming, write Salla Tuomivaara and Siri Martinsen.

Salla Tuomivaara is the director of Animalia and Siri Martinsen, veterinarian, is the director of NOAH. They are the co-authors of the report *Nordic fur trade – marketed as responsible business*.

For the second year running, the European fur industry recently pimped its products at a lavishly organised exhibition in the European Parliament. This was an unashamed attempt to mainstream this morally questionable trade.

'Member states have an opportunity to play a leading role for animal welfare globally by phasing out fur farming'

The Nordic countries, in particular, have been doing their utmost to brand their fur industry as being of high quality in terms of animal welfare. Finnish-owned Saga Furs, one of the main players in the European fur industry, has been involved in working against animal welfare improvements in several countries. The fur industry's attitude towards animal welfare is very different from what is publicly expressed.

Fur farming and its animal welfare problems are the same everywhere, in Finland as well as in Denmark and China. Active predators such as minks and foxes, the main species reared on fur farms, are kept in long rows of battery wire mesh cages where their behavioural needs cannot be met.

The solitary mink is kept in close vicinity to other animals. Swimming and hunting are significant aspects of the species' lifestyle. In the wild, these animals move over large territories that always stretch along waterways. The species of fox that is kept on fur farms also moves over large territories in the wild. Yet imprisoned in wire mesh cages, these animals are denied the ability to express their species' specific behaviour, such as running, playing and digging.

Is European fur produced under strict animal welfare regulations as the fur industry claims? The answer is no. In fact, in the European countries with the highest animal welfare standards for animals kept for fur production, fur farming is either forbidden or the wire mesh battery cages have been phased out. The UK for example banned fur farming over a decade ago.

If you happened to pass by the fur industry's exhibition, you may have been given the impression that the fur industry themselves is improving animal welfare through the development of their own animal-based welfare indicators; a scheme known as WelFur.

The truth is that WelFur does not address the welfare problems associated with the confined cage environment, as highlighted by the European Commission's Scientific Committee on Animal Health and Animal Welfare: "Since current husbandry systems cause serious problems for all species of animals reared for fur, efforts should be made for all species to design housing systems which fulfil the needs of the animals."

Studies aimed at improving housing conditions have, on the whole, been conceived and conducted within the framework of the standard cage environment. This is also the problem with the fur industry's own animal welfare indicators – they are based upon the wire mesh battery cage systems of today. WelFur seems more like a project aimed at validating fur farming as a means of livelihood, rather than at developing better welfare conditions for the animals.

'Is European fur produced under strict regulations as the fur industry claims? The answer is no'

Any significant improvements in animal welfare, such as possibilities for mink to swim and for foxes to express important natural behaviour through digging, would mean unprofitability for the fur industry. The fur industry is, therefore, working hard to keep conditions on fur farms as they are, with the animals paying the price.

'We believe the animals' needs should be respected – that is what animal welfare is all about'

A variety of opinion polls conducted across Europe indicate that the opposition towards fur farming is strong. In Belgium and Germany, 86 per cent are against fur farming and 78 per cent of Swedes think that fur farming should be banned. In Italy, 91 per cent of those polled stated that they are opposed to fur farming.

EU member states have an opportunity to play a leading role for animal welfare globally by phasing out fur farming. We call upon the members of the European Parliament to support national bans on fur farming in the member states.

There is sufficient independent scientific evidence that the raising of active carnivorous animals, such as mink and fox, in small wire mesh battery cages seriously compromises animal welfare. The European fur industry chooses to overlook the fact that the report considers recent scientific studies, including some of those funded by the fur industry. These studies confirm that animal welfare is compromised on fur farms.

The Norwegian Veterinary Association stated earlier this year that it "regards today's fur farming as clearly incompatible with the demands in the Animal Welfare Act (...) The animal welfare in fur farming has shown little improvement over the last 15 years, despite the use of disproportionally large official resources both on research and inspection, compared with other animal husbandry."

It is correct that we do not believe that animals should be raised in small cages for a luxury product nobody needs. We believe the animals' needs should be respected – that is what animal welfare is all about.

21 October 2015

⇨ The above information is reprinted with kind permission from EurActiv.com. Please visit www.euractiv.com for further information.

Distinctions must be made between ideology and animal welfare

By Kenneth Ingman and Mette Lykke Nielsen, Fur Europe

Animal welfare is not the true motive behind activist crusades against the fur industry? it is ideology wrapped in sheep's clothing, write Kenneth Ingman and Mette Lykke Nielsen.

Kenneth Ingman and Mette Lykke Nielsen are chairman and head of public affairs respectively at Fur Europe. They wrote in reply to an opinion article by animal rights groups Animalia and NOAH, published previously by EurActiv.

The two animal rights groups, Animalia and Norwegian NOAH, are the authors behind the report *Nordic Fur Trade – marketed as responsible business* that was presented by Eurogroup4Animals in the European Parliament on 15 October.

The report brings nothing new to the already highly polarised debate over fur. The premise for claiming poor welfare in the European fur sector remains that fur-farmed species are deprived the opportunity to exercise natural behaviour and suffer as a consequence. This either expresses a political motivation to ban fur farming by imposing economically unsustainable conditions on fur farmers (large territories and swimming water would be required), or it expresses the ideological idea that animal farms must 100% mirror nature to morally justify the keeping of animals.

The latter is a legitimate philosophical view, but in terms of animal welfare – a concept that can be measured, weighed and proved – the claim that the domesticated fur-farmed species suffer in the existing housing systems falls short. There is plenty of internationally published research confirming that fur-farmed species do exercise natural behaviour. The farmed mink, for example, spends 70–80% of its time in its nest box, mates naturally and raises its own cubs, which precisely reflects the behaviour of its wild counterpart.

Unfortunately, Eurogroup4Animals and its members take a one-sided focus on natural behaviour as the only relevant welfare parameter. This is rather disrespectful to the animal-science community, where the existing consensus holds that the best way to assess animal welfare is through a multifactorial approach.

HOW THE ANIMAL ACTIVISTS WOULD LIKE TO BE SEEN

HOW THE FUR INDUSTRY SEES THEM

Species-specific behaviour is a part of a multifactorial approach, but cannot constitute animal welfare alone, unless one holds the philosophical view that 'good' equals nature. From a scientific point of view, the weight given to species-specific behaviour in agricultural housing systems must, however, be established with scientific facts, and not romantic assumptions about how life in the wild might be.

As Eurogroup4Animals has done before, Animalia and NOAH also refer to a report stemming from the European Commission's Scientific Committee on Animal Health and Animal Welfare (SCAHAW) for scientific guidance.

The publishing of the report caused a furore in Brussels in 2001, as six of the eight scientists who formed the working group issued a protest letter stating, "The report is politically slanted against fur farming. Large numbers of references have been removed and it contains several errors of fact or interpretation, some of which are so ridiculous that they compromise the report's credibility."

The Commission acknowledged the obvious professional problems of the report by adding a 14-page erratum, with more than 300 missing references to the European Commission's website.

Science is indeed important and acknowledging the existence of societal concerns over animal welfare in the fur sector, Fur Europe has voluntarily initiated the WelFur programme for fur-farmed species. Based on the principles of the European Commission's Welfare Quality project, WelFur is a farm-level certification programme designed to assess animal welfare on a scientific basis, offer tools to improve animal welfare and provide consumer transparency.

WelFur is not a marketing tactic either. The programme is developed by independent scientists from seven European universities, and it is based on the so-called animal indicators wherever possible; the closest we get to asking the animals themselves how they feel. It is somewhat of a weird feeling to voluntarily introduce a world-leading animal-welfare programme, based on all existing scientific research available, yet still be accused of white washing animal welfare standards.

The explanation may well lie in the ideological views of Animalia and NOAH, as both organisations openly pursue a society free of animal use. It is much more of a mystery why Eurogroup4Animals, an otherwise respected animal lobby organisation working to improve animal welfare in the EU, is willing to let the rather radical philosophy of animal liberation hijack their agenda.

Fur farming was on the programme when Eurogroup4Animals hosted an event in the European Parliament in October 2014, but Fur Europe was not invited. Likewise, we were not invited when the report *Nordic Fur Trade* was presented on 15 October this year. In addition, Eurogroup4Animals refused to publicly debate with the fur sector, when we invited them to discuss issues over animal welfare and ethics during the European fur sector's 'This is Fur' event in the European Parliament less than four weeks ago.

Rumours are that the European fur production will be discussed at the next meeting of the Intergroup on the Welfare and Conservation of Animals in Strasbourg in November. With Eurogroup4Animals working as the secretariat for the Intergroup, Fur Europe looks forward to receiving an invitation.

It is a precondition for the democratic conversation that all parties are being invited to the table, and Fur Europe is willing to discuss any issue related to animal welfare or ethics with any stakeholder around. However, it certainly appears as though the only interest Eurogroup4Animals and other animal lobby groups have is to keep the fur debate polarised. The purpose of this strategy seems to be to avoid dealing with actual facts and stigmatise fur. Animal welfare is not the issue; apparently it is the sheer existence of fur.

The real marketing trick in the debate over fur is to take an ideology and disguise it as animal welfare before presenting it to the public.

28 October 2015

⇨ The above information is reprinted with kind permission from EurActiv.com. Please visit www.euractiv.com for further information.

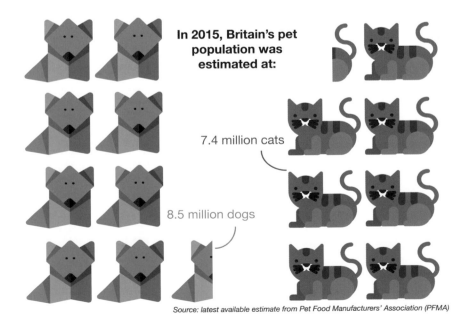

In 2015, Britain's pet population was estimated at:

7.4 million cats

8.5 million dogs

Source: latest available estimate from Pet Food Manufacturers' Association (PFMA)

Why we use animals in research

From the Medical Research Council.

Animals are used to gain understanding of some cell structures and physiological and pathological processes. Although their physiology doesn't identically mimic the human body, they act as 'models' for studying human disease, and are used to develop new treatments for diseases.

Much basic research (research on physiological, pathological and therapeutic processes rather than on people) also requires the use of animals in experiments. Such research has provided – and continues to provide – the essential foundation for improvements in medical and veterinary knowledge, education and practice. Many of the developments achieved through the use of animals have also benefited farm, domestic and wild animals, helping them to live longer and healthier lives.

While alternative techniques cannot always reproduce the complexity of a living creature, we only fund the use of animals when there is no alternative research technique and where the expected benefits of the research outweigh the effects.

The MRC will only fund research using animals where:

⇨ No viable non-animal alternatives exist

⇨ The research is fully compliant with current Home Office legislation

⇨ The research is approved by a local ethics committee

⇨ The research has been successfully independently peer-reviewed

⇨ The researchers have properly considered all the replacement, refinement or reduction of the animals in the experiment.

The researchers have demonstrated that they are using the correct animal model and the statistically correct number of animals to make sure that the research is of the highest quality possible.

Animals are certainly not a perfect model for humans and scientists are working to find alternatives. There have been many advances in this area and replacements for animal modelsopens in new window are being developed all the time. Most researchers would far prefer not to use animals in their work but most appreciate the necessity of doing so. The MRC is proud of the developments that have come about through using animals in research we have funded.

3Rs: Replacement, refinement and reduction

The MRC plays an active role in developing and disseminating the principles of the 3Rs (replacement, refinement and reduction):

Replacement

Replacement refers to methods that avoid or replace the use of animals defined as 'protected' under the Animals (Scientific Procedures) Act 1986 (ASPA) in an area where they would otherwise have been used. 'Protected' animals are all living vertebrates -except man and cephalopods, such as the octopus

Replacement methods can be absolute replacements - techniques which do not involve animals at any point, such as computer modelling, in vitro methodologies (e.g. tissue engineering), or human volunteers - or relative replacements, which avoid or replace the use of 'protected' animals with organisms not protected under ASPA, such as Drosophila (flies) or worms.

Growing 'mini-brains' from stem-cells

An example of Replacement in practice

Dr Madeline Lancaster and her team at MRC Laboratory of Molecular Biology employ cerebral organoids, also known as 'mini brains', grown from pluripotent stem cells to model human brain development in vitro. Using in vitro models has the potential to capture the intricacies of the human brain more accurately than animals, which do not have the anatomical and functional complexity of human brains. The challenge with using in vitro models has been to model the whole brain and its complex functions, rather than single cell types or processes individually. Using brain organoids is a way of overcoming this.

The process for growing these 3D tissues was first described in a paper by Dr Lancaster and colleagues published in Nature in September 2013. Her team has previously focussed on modelling neurodevelopmental disorders, such as microcephaly, a disorder characterized by a significantly reduced brain size (some cases may be associated with Zika virus infection). Her work is currently concentrated on other neurodevelopmental disorders such as autism and intellectual disability, by introducing mutations seen in these disorders into the cells used to make the organoids. This will give us a further understanding of the role these mutations play in the development of these conditions. The cerebral organoids are a major step towards reducing reliance on animals in studying neurological diseases and the development of new treatments, and have already been up taken by 16 other research laboratories. The paper authored by Dr Lancaster, who has recently given a TEDx talk about her researchopens in new window, won the 2015 NC3R's 3Rs Prize for outstanding published research with 3Rs impact.

Refinement

Refinement refers to improvements to scientific procedures and husbandry which minimise actual or potential pain, suffering, distress or lasting harm and/or improve animal welfare in situations where the use of animals is unavoidable. It applies to the lifetime experience of the animal. There is evidence that refinement not only benefits animals, but can also improve the quality of research findings.

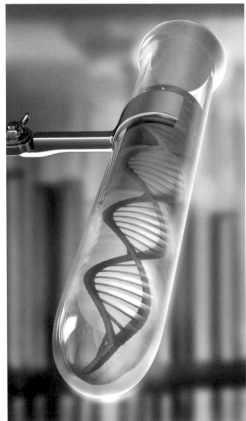

Post-surgical care

An example of Refinement in practice

Dr Simon Milling's lab at the University of Glasgow aim to better understand the adaptive immune responses against infections in the intestine, to help manage inflammatory bowel diseases and food allergies. It is thought that specialised dendritic cells, which travel from the intestine to the lymph nodes, are important in mediating these responses, but they can often only be obtained via surgical procedures. In addition to replacing the use of larger animals to surgically collect these cells, Dr Milling's team have worked hard to refine the surgical cannulation technique in mice. Improvements in the surgical management of the mice have enabled larger volumes of lymph to be collected after surgery, and improved post-operative procedures and the use of a thoracic harness have enabled cannulated animals the full range of normal movement, within their normal cages. This also prevents the need for restraint in the post-surgical period. The three published papers using these refined techniques have been cited over 100 times in the last three years, and staff from laboratories in the UK, Sweden, and the USA have been trained to use the refined procedures.

Reduction

Reduction refers to methods which minimise animal use and enable researchers to obtain comparable levels of information from fewer animals or to obtain more information from the same number of animals, thereby reducing the future use of animals.

The National Centre for the Replacement, Refinement and Reduction of Animals in Research (NC3Rs)

The MRC is a major funder of The National Centre for the Replacement, Refinement and Reduction of Animals in Research (NC3Rs)opens in new window, a scientific organisation which leads the discovery, development

and promotion of new ways to replace, reduce and refine the use of animals in research and testing (the 3Rs). The NC3Rs is the UK's major sponsor of 3Rs research. The NC3Rs have issued various guidance documents, and provide an extensive library of 3Rs resources.

3Rs impact in MRC funded research

Currently, about one third of MRC–funded research programmes involve the use of animals under the Animals (Scientific Procedures) Actopens in new window. Each year, the MRC collects information from its researchers on how they have implemented 3Rs in their work via the evaluation tool, Researchfish. Some examples of how researchers implement the 3Rs in practice include:

⇨ The reduction of animal numbers through better experimental design

⇨ Replacement of specific procedures with alternatives or non-animal technology

⇨ Substitution by a species of lower neurophysiological sensitivity

⇨ Enhancement of animal welfare and enrichment.

Around a third of MRC-funded researchers proposing to use animals in their research reported making additional changes to further reduce, refine or replace animal use during the course of their project. Furthermore, around 15% were able to refine or develop methodology with 3Rs impact that could be shared/adopted by others.

⇨ The above information is reprinted with kind permission from the Medical Research Council. Please visit www.mrc.ac.uk for further information.

Number of animal experiments continues to rise in UK

Surge in genetic research sees number of procedures increase again despite government pledge to limit their use.

By Haroon Siddique

The number of scientific experiments using animals continued to increase last year despite the Coalition's commitment to work to reduce their use, official figures show.

There were 4.12 million scientific procedures using animals in Great Britain in 2013, a rise of 0.3% on the previous year, according to Home Office statistics, following an upward trend that has seen the number increase by 1.41 million since 1995.

Animal welfare groups criticised the figures but the head of the Home Office's Animals in Science Regulation Unit (ASRU) insisted progress was being made towards the Coalition's 2010 commitment.

"There are enormous efforts going on to not using animals where it's unnecessary for them to be used," said Dr Judy MacArthur Clark. "Where these animals are being used, then there's a necessity for that use. There's a lot of effort going into replacement."

She said the figures did not show the number of experiments using animals that had been avoided because of work to reduce animal use. Under the law, scientists are required to consider the 3Rs: to replace the use of animals; reduce the number need; or refine procedures to cause less suffering.

In only one year (2009) since 2001 has the number of experiments on animals fallen on the previous 12 months. The lastest increase has been driven by a rise in the number of procedures undertaken to breed genetically modified animals (GM) and animals with a harmful genetic mutation (HM), which, in total, rose 6% to 2.1 million last year and has risen by 573% since 1995. By contrast, the number of experiments for other purposes fell 5% to 2.02 million last year, its lowest level in two decades.

The Home Office said that "while many types of research have declined or even ended, the advent of modern scientific techniques has opened up new research areas, with genetically modified animals, mainly mice, often being required to support those areas".

Professor Roger Morris, former academic manager of King's College London's experimental animal facility, said that modified animals were needed for modelling the early stages of complex diseases such as cancer, Parkinson's disease and dementia, more accurately than before.

After breeding to produce GM or HM animals, the most common purposes for experiments were fundamental biological research and research into the development of and quality control of drugs or devices.

The ASRU found 33 issues of non-compliance last year, including the death of 1,000 rats and mice at an unnamed breeding establishment. MacArthur Clark said that while such incidents should be avoided, they must be seen in the context of the total number of animals used.

Michelle Thew, chief executive of the British Union for the Abolition of Vivisection, said: "The Government has now failed for a third year on its 2010 post-election pledge to work to reduce the number of animals used in research and, as a result, millions of animals continue to suffer and die in our laboratories."

Peta described GM experiments as "imprecise, inefficient and unreliable 'Frankenstein science'".

10 July 2014

⇨ The above information is reprinted with kind permission from *The Guardian*. Please visit www.theguardian.com for further information.

Are animal experiments necessary and can they be justified?

Animal experiments are one of the traditional approaches to studying how human and animal bodies work (in health and illness) and for testing medicines and chemicals.

Scientists who use animals argue that there is currently no other way to achieve their scientific objectives, and that any pain or distress caused to the animals is outweighed by the potential benefits of their research.

However, 'necessity' and 'justification' are both matters of opinion and open to debate. There is a range of views on how much suffering should be allowed and for what purpose (e.g. aiming to treat cancer, drug addiction or male pattern baldness, to assess the safety of a new industrial chemical, or to find out how birds navigate) and to what species of animal.

The UK law that controls animal experiments is supposed to reflect this. It requires that the likely harms to the animals are weighed against the potential benefits of the project, that there are no alternatives available, and that the numbers and suffering of animals are minimised.

This provides a framework for making decisions about animal experiments, but the system should be implemented more effectively. For example, it is often suggested that most animal experiments are "life-saving" medical research and are all done to the "highest possible standards". But sweeping statements like these do not stand up to scrutiny, for two main reasons:

There is serious debate within the scientific community about the value of information obtained from many animal tests, and about the relevance of various animal 'models'. This raises doubts about the scientific validity of applying the results from research on animals to humans.

There are many concerns about the poor quality of much animal research.

The issues relating to scientific validity and quality are deeply worrying. Research that is of little value, poorly designed or conducted, and badly reported is a waste of animals' lives, causing suffering that should have been entirely avoidable. Animal experiments like these are certainly neither necessary nor justified.

Efforts are at last beginning to be made to recognise and address these problems, and the concerns do not apply to all scientists and research areas. However, poor quality animal research continues to be funded, licensed, carried out and published. This should stop.

What we think

⇨ The scientific community, including researchers, funding bodies, journal editors and the Home Office, should do much more to critically review the scientific validity of animal experiments.

⇨ The 'need' to use animals, and the justification for the suffering caused, should both be challenged much more strongly. Animals' lives and welfare should be given higher priority.

⇨ Badly designed and poorly carried out experiments are invalid science and waste animals' lives. They should not be licensed by the Home Office, given grants by funding bodies or published in scientific journals.

⇨ Even scientifically valid research may not add significantly to knowledge in its field, or it may only be of interest to a few people. This does not justify harming animals.

⇨ Decisions about animal use are largely made by scientists, for scientists – a wider range of perspectives should be involved.

⇨ We want to see an end to animal suffering in the name of science. A more humane approach is needed.

⇨ The above information is reprinted with kind permission from the RSPCA. Please visit www.rspca.org.uk for further information.

How well informed do you feel, if at all, about the use of animals in scientific research in the UK?

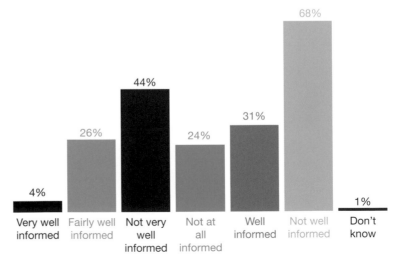

Very well informed	4%	
Fairly well informed	26%	
Not very well informed	44%	
Not at all informed	24%	
Well informed	31%	
Not well informed	68%	
Don't know	1%	

Source: Ipsos Mori, BIS Animal Testing Questionnaire, 2014

How do we weigh the moral value of human lives against animal ones?

An article from **The Conversation.**

THE CONVERSATION

By Daniel Crimston, PhD Candidate in Psychology, The University of Queensland; Brock Bastian, ARC Future Fellow, Melbourne School of Psychological Sciences, University of Melbourne; Matthew Hornsey, Professor Paul Bain, Lecturer in Psychology, Queensland University of Technology

Imagine a unique set of scales that measures the value of life. If a single human were on one side, how many chimpanzees (our closest genetic relatives) would need to be on the other side before the scales tipped in their direction?

This may seem like an abstract, irrelevant or even offensive question to some people. But it was made horrifically real by the death last week of Harambe, the Cincinnati Zoo gorilla who was shot after a young boy fell into his enclosure.

Zoo handlers were faced with the agonising decision to take Harambe's life to ensure the young boy would not lose his. The response to this event online has varied from anger, to sadness, through to considerations of how much choice the zoo's staff really had. How do we decide what our own lives are worth compared with other species?

Perhaps we can try to frame the comparison in relative terms. There are 7.4 billion human beings on the planet, whereas Western lowland gorillas are critically endangered. Does a human life hold more value than that of a member of a critically endangered animal species?

Harambe's death suggests that the instinctive answer is yes, but is there a point at which some people's moral scales might tip the other way? Our research suggests there might be.

The concept of 'moral expansion'

No one expects an easy answer to this question. But the fact that we can even ask it shows that our moral sensibilities have expanded beyond the boundaries of our own species.

Many of us feel a deep moral responsibility not just to protect our fellow humans, but to guard the moral rights of entities the world over. This change, which has spanned the past few centuries, has resulted in some serious ethical challenges to the ways we interact with other species and the environment.

Recently, animal rights organisations in the United States have fought for the legal personhood status of chimpanzees like Tommy, while animal advocates have petitioned the United Nations for a Declaration of the Rights of Great Apes since 1993.

In the meantime, a river in New Zealand has been officially granted legal personhood status (similar to the status given to corporations), making the river a legal 'person' with its own rights and interests under law.

In line with the concept of compassionate conservation, these examples highlight the narrowing of the gulf between the moral rights of humans, non-humans and the environment.

For supporters of these causes, human rights and corresponding moral standing should no longer be restricted to humans.

Are you willing to sacrifice?

The legal semantics are interesting, but what about when it really comes to the crunch? Our recent research has examined how widely people spread their moral concern to others. We found that this is a key predictor of the type of moral decision-making that compares the value of a human life to that of another animal.

We asked people the following question: how many other human beings would need to be in danger before you sacrificed your own life to ensure their survival? But our research didn't stop at humans.

We also asked how many chimpanzees would need to be at risk. How many ants? How many redwood trees?

Responses to these questions were as varied as the responses to the shooting of Harambe.

Some people said they would sacrifice their life if it meant that just a few chimpanzees would keep theirs.

Others said it wouldn't matter how many animals or trees were in danger; a human life was simply worth more.

We found that we could predict people's responses to specific questions based on their position on what we call the "moral expansiveness scale". Those whose moral outlook stretched further beyond humans were more likely to say they would sacrifice themselves to benefit other animals or nature.

A moral dilemma

Human beings are becoming increasingly morally expansive. As a species we are adopting a moral standard that represents ethical and altruistic responsibilities on a global scale. This is reflected in the extension of human rights to chimpanzees and the granting of legal rights to elements of our natural environment.

However, this trend is accompanied by an escalating moral conflict. The extension of our moral boundaries is happening just as the global human population is growing exponentially, leading to tension and competition over scarce resources.

As a consequence, we are increasingly likely to face ethical dilemmas over the value of human versus non-human life. It won't be in the form of a quick decision to kill an animal to save the life of a child. These dilemmas will play out in courtrooms and parliaments, as human needs are pitted against environmental ones, and as the battle for natural resources brings threats of deforestation and species extinction.

As we edge ever closer to the brink of the Earth's sixth mass extinction, perhaps we need to consider just exactly what a human life is worth.

8 June 2016

⇨ The above information is reprinted with kind permission from *The Conversation*. Please visit www.theconversation.com for further information.

Global polls reveal consumers worldwide want an end to animal testing for cosmetics

We knew that there was strong support for a global ban on cosmetics animal testing – and decisive action to replace it with non-animal alternatives – and now we have the scientific proof. HSI and our #BeCrueltyFree campaign partners commissioned a series of public opinion surveys in some of the world's key cosmetics markets – Brazil, Canada and South Korea – while The Humane Society of the United States commissioned a U.S. poll. HSI also partnered with LUSH Fresh Handmade Cosmetics and local animal welfare organisations to commission polls in Japan and Taiwan.

Here's what we found

Canada: eight out of ten people support a national cosmetics animal testing ban

⇨ 88 per cent agreed that animal testing "can cause pain and suffering to animals and it is not worth causing this kind of suffering just to test the safety of cosmetics, especially when there are safe ingredients already available".

⇨ 81 percent support a nationwide ban on the testing of cosmetics and their ingredients on animals.

⇨ Among those who were either undecided or opposed to a Canadian ban, when told that the European Union has banned cosmetic testing on animals, a third changed their minds to support a Canadian ban.

South Korea: seven out of ten people support a national animal testing ban for cosmetics

⇨ 65.6 per cent agree that animal testing "can cause pain and suffering to animals and it is not worth causing this kind of suffering just to test the safety of cosmetics, especially when there are safe ingredients already available".

⇨ 70.2 per cent support a nationwide ban on the testing of cosmetics and their ingredients on animals.

⇨ Among those who were initially undecided or opposed, nearly half changed their minds to support a Korean ban after learning that the EU and Israel have already banned cosmetic testing on animals.

Brazil: Two out of three people support a national ban

⇨ Two out of three Brazilians support a nationwide ban on the testing of cosmetics and their ingredients on animals.

⇨ 61 per cent agreed that animal testing "can cause pain and suffering to animals and it is not worth causing this kind of suffering just to test the safety of cosmetics, especially when there are safe ingredients already available".

⇨ Two out of three agreed that "cosmetic companies that say they are committed to sustainability, protection of the environment and use of natural or organic ingredients should also ensure that they do not test their products on animals".

Japan (source: LUSH Japan)

⇨ Nearly 90 per cent responded that "I don't want manufacturers to use ingredients in cosmetics whose safety cannot be determined unless they are tested on animals."

- More than half said they felt strongly about the issue of cosmetics testing on animals.

- 65 per cent said that "manufactures that test on animals should publicise the species and number of animals that they use for testing".

Taiwan (source: Taiwan SPCA)

- 76.5 per cent believe animals shouldn't suffer in the name of beauty.

- 69.2 per cent of Taiwanese consumers want to see cosmetics testing on animals banned.

United States (source: HSUS)

- 68 per cent know that animals are used to test the safety of cosmetics.

- Three in four voters say that they would feel safer, or as safe, if non-animal methods were used to test the safety of a cosmetic instead of animal testing.

- Strong majorities of women, regardless of age, level of education or ethnicity, think animal testing of cosmetics should be illegal.

27 January 2016

- From *Global Polls Reveal Consumers Wordwide Want an End to Animal Testing for Cosmetics.* Copyright © 2016 Humane Society International.

Cosmetics testing: the animal ban spreads

FRAME is delighted that more and more countries are starting processes to bring an end to cosmetics testing on animals. It has been against the law to test cosmetics or their ingredients on animals in the EU since the start of 2013. Crucially, it is also illegal to market cosmetics that have undergone animal tests elsewhere.

That means manufacturers around the world have had to produce products for sale in the EU market without resorting to animal use, and the trend has led to other countries' decisions to phase out old animal-based safety assessments. The latest countries to join the move away from animal tests are Japan, the US, and Canada.

Japanese law does not require animal-based tests on cosmetics, but there is no prohibition either, so individual companies test in whatever way they see fit. The growth of European products in the Japanese market means that customers have been exposed to so-called 'cruelty free' products and there is now a growing demand for home produced cosmetics that meet the same standards.

In the past Japan has made pledges to raise its standards in animal welfare and environmental protection. In 2014 the European Business Council in Japan called on its government to honour that commitment, including the introduction on validated alternatives to animal testing wherever possible.

A similar situation exists in the US. The law does not require or ban animal tests on cosmetics or their ingredients, but a bill, the Humane Cosmetics Act HR 2858, is currently going through the US legislature, led by Representative Martha McSally of Arizona. The bill would require all animal-based cosmetics tests to be phased out within a year of its adoption. It would prevent: "The internal or external application or exposure of any cosmetic to the skin,

eyes, or other body part of a live non-human vertebrate for purposes of evaluating the safety or efficacy of a cosmetic."

Current legislation in Canada requires that all cosmetic products are "safe when used as intended", but does not specify animal testing. However, the Food and Drugs Act, which covers the subject, does not prohibit animal tests. Now Senator Carolyn Stewart Olsen of New Brunswick has proposed an amendment that would introduce a ban on tests being carried out in Canada, and on the sale of products that have been tested elsewhere.

Other countries where the topic is under discussion include Australia, Brazil, South Korea and Taiwan.

FRAME Scientific Director Dr Gerry Kenna said: "FRAME is delighted that the ban on testing cosmetics on animals is spreading around the world. There are many valid alternative methods now available that do not require the use of animals so there is no excuse for the practice to continue anywhere. We hope this trend continues to grow."

In the UK, a cosmetic product is defined as "any substance or mixture intended to be placed in contact with various external parts of the human body" and intended for cleaning, perfuming or changing their appearance. This includes skin, hair, teeth, and nails. The exact definitions may differ in detail in other countries but are broadly similar.

13 November 2015

- The above information is reprinted with kind permission from FRAME. Please visit www.frame.org.uk for further information.

Key facts

- Under the Animal Welfare Act 2006, powers exist for secondary legislation and codes of practice to be made to promote the welfare of animals. (page 1)

- The Pet Animals Act 1951 (as amended in 1983) – this act protects the welfare of animals sold as pets. It requires any person keeping a pet shop to be licensed by the local council. (page 1)

- 93,424 animals were imported into the UK in 2015 for commercial and non-commercial reasons. (page 3)

- 33,249 animals were imported into the UK in 2015 from Ireland, Lithuania, Hungary, Poland and Romania – that's up 75% (14,339) from 18,910 in 2014. (page 3)

- A report released by Battersea Dogs and Cats Home in October 2015 revealed how the unregulated breeding industry was putting dogs at risk. The report showed that less than 12% of puppies in the UK are bred by licensed breeders, meaning that dogs could be sold from unsuitable premises, long before they are ready to leave their mothers. (page 4)

- In 2014-2015, more than 7,200 bulls and steers (castrated bull calves) were killed by bullfighters across Spain, the news website El Diario reports. (page 5)

- In 2014, Denmark banned kosher and halal slaughter as minister says "animal rights come before religion". (page 6)

- The specific offence of dog fighting does not exist in the UK; it is contained within the broader offence of animal fighting prohibited under Section 8 of the Animal Welfare Act with a maximum penalty of 51 weeks in prison. By contrast, in the US dog fighting is a felony offence in all 50 states with a maximum penalty of several years in prison. (page 9)

- 25 million birds are illegally slaughtered in the Mediterranean every year. (page 9)

- More than 30 countries around the world have restricted the use of wild animals in circuses. (page 10)

- By 75% to 11%, British people say keeping monkeys as pets should be banned. (page 11)

- Globally, 70-80% of egg-laying hens are kept in battery cages. (page 12)

- Pet obesity – the facts: Over 5.5 million pets – more than 3.3 million dogs, 2 million cats and 168,000 rabbits – are given daily treats. (page 19)

- 88% of owners believe overweight pets have a shorter lifespan and 60% of owners think overweight pets are less happy. (page 19)

- 94.5% believed a ban on the use of wild animals in travelling circuses was the best option to achieve consistently better welfare standards for these animals. (page 26)

- Lions are reportedly already extinct in 25 African countries and close to extinction in ten others, with numbers across the continent estimated at just 15,000 – 20,000 compared to around 200,000 in the 1980s. (page 27)

- A scientific study published in 2007 after the Randomised Badger Culling Trial, which was conducted over nine years, concluded: "badger culling cannot meaningfully contribute to the future control of cattle TB in Britain". (page 28)

- In Belgium and Germany, 86 per cent are against fur farming and 78 per cent of Swedes think that fur farming should be banned. In Italy, 91 per cent of those polled stated that they are opposed to fur farming. (page 30)

- Animals are used in research to gain understanding of some cell structures and physiological and pathological processes. Although their physiology doesn't identically mimic the human body, they act as 'models' for studying human disease, and are used to develop new treatments for diseases. (page 33)

- There were 4.12 million scientific procedures using animals in Great Britain in 2013, a rise of 0.3% on the previous year, according to Home Office statistics, following an upward trend that has seen the number increase by 1.41 million since 1995. (page 35)

- In the United States, 68 per cent know that animals are used to test the safety of cosmetics. However, three in four voters say that they would feel safer, or as safe, if non-animal methods were used to test the safety of a cosmetic instead of animal testing. (page 39)